FAMILY THERAPY
AND
SOCIAL CHANGE

Dedicated to my family: Marilyn, Lisa, Andy,
Mildred, Frances,
Susan, Marty, Pamela, David, Meredith,
Sam, Phoebe, George,
   and to uncles, aunts, cousins, and other
relatives shaping history past/present/future.

4 JOB 523   -0000-04 SOLO CHANGE-17 D1-2

REV:12-13 EXP:12-10 BG SIZ: 171.01

FAMILY THERAPY
AND
SOCIAL CHANGE

by
NEIL M. SOLOMON

SCHOOL OF
CALIFORNIA PROFESSIONAL
PSYCHOLOGY
LOS ANGELES

IRVINGTON PUBLISHERS, INC.
551 FIFTH AVENUE NEW YORK, N.Y. 10017

Library of Congress Cataloging in Publication Data
Solomon, Neil 1932–
   Family therapy and social change.

   Bibliography: p.
   Includes index.
   1. Family psychotherapy. 2. Social change.
3. Feminism. I. Title.
RC488.5.S64   616.8′915   79-20505
ISBN 0-8290-0088-7

Acknowledgments

Most of the work for this book was completed through the Humanistic Psychology Institute in San Francisco, a free-standing graduate institution where I studied as a research fellow for the Ph.D. in psychology. Special recognition goes first and foremost to Richard Farson, professor of psychology, who guided and inspired me through every painstaking phase of the project.

Next, I must thank my two field faculty chairpeople, Drs. Pierre Ventur and Don-David Lusterman, who remained on call for the duration of the program.

Michelle Berdy provided me with her extraordinary talents as a critic and line-by-line editor. At my lowest point, her reassurance that the entire manuscript could be reorganized came to fruition as we worked long hours rewriting.

Linda J. LaRosa is another friend who dropped her own writing projects to serve as a grammarian for many sections of the transcribed audiotapes.

Special kudos to Deborah Tax who had the assignment of typing a sometimes illegible manuscript.

There were many other contributors and to each of them I am grateful.

Neil Solomon

Foreword

Family therapists and interested lay people are concerned with the stressful changes happening to the modern nuclear family. Certainly the family institution, like all institutions, is not immune to evolution. However, when change has been avoided for centuries, a violent revolution results. The family institution, in the wake of women's liberation and the heightened consciousness of men and children, is finding itself in chaotic flux. Yet, professionals in the field of family therapy are disturbed by the blanket pronouncements of social radicals and extremists that the nuclear family faces an imminent demise. *Family Therapy and Social Change* is a refreshing demonstration that modern issues like women's liberation and individual consciousness raising can be handled within the family structure in a constructive manner from which each member may profit.

This book explains that the family can learn much by redefining the position of woman, wife, and mother. I have always maintained that women will not be liberated solely through legislation and equal employment opportunities – although these are significant steps. When the role of the female has been examined and redefined within the family structure, the liberation of husbands and children will follow. In this volume the changing attitudes of father, mother, and child are scrutinized from the standpoint of incurring the satisfaction of the individual while stabilizing the family unit as a whole. The families profiled here are real. Readers will recognize themselves somewhere within these presentations.

Family Therapy and Social Change is a theoretical work, yet its examples are concrete, its conclusions pragmatic. Neil Solomon has contributed a trenchant overview and compassionate understanding of the nuclear family at an evolutionary crossroad.

by Thomas S. Fogarty, M.D.

Preface

This book presents an evolving model for change in family therapy. The impetus for developing a new model was an outgrowth of separate but related changes in the field of family therapy resulting from transformations in the larger social order, specifically, the development of the communications model and the resurgence of feminism.

Conceptualizations of psychopathology have recently shifted from intrapsychic and psychodynamic paradigms to an interpersonal communication model. More recently, the emerging women's liberation movement caused changes in the power relationships between men and women. Pressures on the traditional nuclear family unit to respond to the reverberations of social change increased as a result of those changes in sexual power relations. Many families, unable to solve their difficulties, turned to family therapy for counseling and assistance. Unfortunately, family therapy, despite its maturation, was rooted in a tradition that saw treatment as synonymous with social adjustment. Historically, social adjustment in American culture has called for differentiated role adjustment, both inside and outside the family system.

Women, who were changing their views of sex roles, demanded new rules by which men and women could live together. The central problem for family therapists became whether or not liberation precluded a family unit. Could the nuclear family adapt to the internal and external pressures?

From this perspective, family therapy and women's consciousness-raising were in opposition. In order to liberate people, feminist writers believed that the nuclear family (along with many other social institutions) must be destroyed or completely transformed. Those committed to the traditional family, faced with the threat of such changes, resisted.

While issues raised by women's studied underscored the strength of the feminist arguments, they did not conform to the theory of systems in human affairs. The intersystemic relationship between people and their social institutions argued for a different conclusion. That is, the liberation of any individual or group requires the reciprocal liberation of those believed to be the oppressors. Men as well as women, children as well as adults, are cast in the dichotomous roles of oppressor and oppressed. The politics of male/female power was not as clearly separable as some women committed to consciousness-raising believed it to be. Rather, liberation and oppression seemed to be more functions of socially determined relationships than of gender or age. Following this line of thought, one could conclude that it is not necessary to disband the nuclear family. In theory, it should be possible to liberate individual family members and still maintain the nuclear family system.

In attempting to find an adequate solution to this dilemma, the writer has integrated two seemingly divergent processes. Consciousness-raising has been incorporated into clinical methods of therapy in order to facilitate the healing of dysfunctional aspects of family life.

Neil Solomon

CONTENTS

Introduction

Family therapy evolved out of a theoretical model within which symptom reduction and behavioral change were contingent upon an intrapsychic and psychodynamic paradigm. The maturation of theory in family therapy represented a shift from individual treatment to the treatment of a family unit. Eventually, family therapy assumed an interpersonal communication model and the entire family was involved in the treatment process.

Symptoms were no longer viewed as a result of intrapsychic disturbance; they were seen as expressions of difficulty within an interpersonal network. An outgrowth of this new theoretical model was that treatment of psychopathology focused attention upon a social unit rather than upon an individual.

As this approach to treatment attained popularity, further observations were made that suggested the possibility that psychopathology within a family unit might be causally related to changes and pressure within the social system itself. In an effort to study this observation, research focused upon the family as an interface between the individual and the larger social institutions that embraced it.

The implications of this research have had an effect upon evolving theoretical models for change. Specifically, it became evident that, indeed, the family was directly influenced by currents of social change to the extent to which problems inside the family were directly related to alterations in the larger social system.

One of the most powerful social changes was the resurgence of feminism. The women's movement pressed for liberation from traditional women's roles. Women began changing their roles inside the family and entered the commercial marketplace in increasing numbers. No longer satisfied with traditional sex role stereotypes, women began to challenge the conventional social structure as they sought to discover new roles within it.

This change brought to the field of family therapy some new and difficult questions. Perhaps the most disquieting was the question of whether the liberation of women was contrary to the maintenance of the traditional nuclear family. Historically, family therapy was dedicated to the conservation of the family system and attempted to achieve a more harmonious adjustment of the family within the larger social system. Shifting women's role did not conform to this paradigm in the sense that liberation pointed to a loosening of social constraints. Moreover, the system's view of human affairs favored the argument that liberation of one person required the reciprocal liberation of others. In this context, were family therapy to continue its dedication to the preservation of the nuclear family, a new theoretical model for liberation and change was necessary.

This book is an attempt to provide family therapy with a theoretical model for liberation and change that favors the conservation of the nuclear family system.

The notion of liberation implies a movement towards change and the opening of new options. Within the nuclear family system this evolves from the passive acquiescence of social constraints that can tie the family into serving economic, political, and social functions of the larger social system. In many cases, a family has been torn apart in its attempts to comply passively with social expectations, particularly when these expectations have run counter to individual and family needs.

Liberation and change within the family is concerned with encouraging a family to examine the forms by which social constraints have been transformed into family life. While it is clear that the social system provides a landscape, a context, in which change can occur, it does not have to circumscribe the manner in which family members must live. Within constraints lies the potentiality for freedom; the family system can function as a vehicle for providing responsible choices, liberation, for its members.

To accomplish this objective, it was necessary to build a theoretical model that could draw upon the existing research in the fields of family theory and behavioral change from both women's consciousness-raising and family therapy.

In Chapter 1, the intersystemic relationship between the nuclear family and the larger social system is examined in order to establish a relationship between social change and changing family structure.

Chapter 2 presents the evolving theoretical and treatment perspectives in the field of family therapy and women's studies. A developmental approach to the literature presents the historical underpinnings of each discipline from its inception to the present time.

In Chapter 3, the development of systems theory in family therapy is combined with the process of socio-political consciousness-raising as a theoretical model for change. Diagrammatic models are presented in an effort to detail the evolving theoretical paradigm of joining consciousness-raising with family therapy. The description of this theoretical model for liberation and change follows with a series of taped therapy transcripts that demonstrate the application of this model in family therapy. Verbatim conversation is accompanied by an analysis of the session presented in a parallel column.

Chapter 4 presents a summary of the work thus far. A discussion of the limitations of a theory and its application concludes the book.

1. The Nuclear Family and the Social Order
An Intersystemic Relationship

THE NUCLEAR FAMILY

Theoretical Perspectives

The concept of the nuclear family is of recent vintage. Many researchers point to early Colonial days in America as the time in which the nuclear family came into existence.[1] A splintered group which broke off from the mainstream extended family forged new territory as a nuclear unit. The nuclear family refers to a family group which consists of two parents and their offspring living together under one roof.[2] Although some contact with extended relatives may persist, the unit is considered nuclear if it exists apart from other kin.

Controversy has surrounded the notion that the nuclear family evolved out of the American Colonial experience. The suggestion that the nuclear family goes much further back in history and might be considered as a "universal human group" is presented in the works of Gough (1959), Kluckhohn (1949), Lowie (1920), Mead (1935), Murdock (1937), Spiro (1960), and Summer and Keller (1927). These writers have cited the biological differences between men and women—the strength of the male, the pregnancy of the female, and the evolving specialized roles due to these differences to support their positions.[3]

A salient question which has emerged from the debate regarding the historical evolution of the nuclear family unit is the extent to which the structure and maintenance of the social system and the nuclear family have become interdependent upon one another for survival. Research pointing to such intersystemic relationship is found in Bell and Vogel (1960); Gibson (1972); Goodman (1972); Group for the Advancement of Psychiatry (1968); Hess and Torney (1967); Howells (1971); Isbister (1973); Kluckhohn (1949); Kaprowski (1973); Landrud (1973); Mace (1974); Millet (1970); Mower (1975); Murdock (1949); Nease, Theron-Stanford (1971); Parsons (1955); Reich (1945); Roszak (1968); Russell (1929); Spiegel (1971); Tec (1975); and Young (1953).

In this context the family is conceptualized as a subsystem of society, and the individual a subsystem of the family (Howell, 1971). In the work of Spiegel (1971), the concept of the family as a subsystem is given considerable attention. The family, according to Spiegel,

can be viewed as a process of transaction involving two foci, such as between the psychological systems of family members and their group interrelations. Or it can be regarded as a process of transaction involving all foci.[4] (p. 58)

Stated another way, Minuchin (1974) writes, "The Family is a social unit that faces a series of developmental tasks." (p. 16.)

It would seem that the idea of a family moving to face developmental tasks, or the family, as a subsystem of the larger society responsive to social change, implies that the nature and form of the family can be conceived of as a socio-cultural artifact. In short, the family unit is not an insulated social group; it is an outgrowth of a larger cultural system and reflects the values intrinsic to that system. The structure of the family and even the relationships and roles and duties of its individual members are determined, to some varying degree, by the prevailing forms of the larger social system.[5]

On the most fundamental level, research indicates that the structure of the nuclear family itself is a rather recent phenomenon, having come into form sometime in the seventeenth century (Aries, 1975). "From this moment on," writes Aries, "the family was completely transformed. Its economic function remained, but educating and socializing functions took precedence."

Historically, it has been suggested that the notion of childhood as a separate stage in the human life cycle did not really evolve until the sixteenth century. Before that time, according to Firestone (1970), Farson (1974), and Aries (1975), childhood was virtually unknown. Attention to childhood as a distinct age group influenced changes in clothing (as a way of denoting social rank), differences in sexuality, and the advent of the modern school. According to Firestone (1970), "with the onset of the child-centered nuclear family, an institution became necessary to structure a 'childhood' that would keep children under the jurisdiction of parents as long as possible[6] Schools multiplied, replacing scholarship and a practical apprenticeship with a theoretical education. The function of these early schools was to 'discipline' children rather than to impart learning for its own sake."[7] (p. 85.)

The growth of industrialization in American society had the effect of sharpening the divisions between adulthood and childhood, as well as adding further to the requirements that both men and women assume clearly demarcated roles. Industrial development was contingent on the family structuring itself along the lines necessary for production in the commercial marketplace.[8] According to Rowbotham (1973),

The family is the place where women work. It also determines the amount of labor which can be released for commodity production, and plays a crucial part in forming consciousness. The family is both essential for capital's reproduction, and a brake on its use of human labor power.

The interrelationship of the structure of the family and the maintenance of the commercial marketplace also receives critical examination in the works of Henry (1965), Marcuse (1964), Millet (1970), Reich (1949), Roszak (1968), and Russell (1929).

"People," explains Marcuse, "recognize themselves in their commodities; they find their soul in their automobile, hi-fi set, split-level home, kitchen equipment . . . the very mechanism which ties the individual to his society has changed, and social control is anchored in the new needs which it has provided."

Following this line of reasoning, we find that the family as a subsystem of the larger society must not only assume a structure in harmony with larger social institutions, but also that many issues and problems inside the family are directly related to the difficulties it faces in maintaining this relationship. Social change, particularly rapid social change, would place considerable stress upon the family to adapt, or fall prey to myriad problems straining family relationships. The problems which arise out of this interface between the family unit and the social structure is of central importance. The strategies, both implicit and explicit, with which the family unit has tried to come to terms with the culture have been varied. There have been a number of studies which suggest that family stress and other related problems are indeed related to the structure and changes in the larger social system.

It has been suggested that the family responds to the commercial marketplace; it would be expected that economic issues would affect family life. In a study conducted by Renee (1970) the relationship between marital satisfaction and socioeconomic status yielded different results between black and white American families. Reports from black families confirmed the belief that they not only rank lower in income levels and education, but report greater dissatisfaction in their marriages than whites. Similarly, census studies by Cowhig (1965), Udry (1967) and Bauman (1967) indicated that the probabilities for achieving stable marriages are greater for whites than for non-whites. Udry (1967) discovered that the lowest marital stability was in the lowest status occupations for men, and the highest stability in the high status occupations. Mercer (1967) found significantly more intact families among whites than among non-whites as well.

Families in which the woman is required to work out of economic necessity have been studied: this research has correlated economic conditions of stress. Axelson (1963) studied reports from husbands and wives in four randomly selected communities in Illinois. These researchers concluded that both partners in marriage ranked lower in marital happiness when economic necessity denied the wife the luxury of choosing whether or not to work and found marriages in greater difficulty when the wife worked full time rather than part time.[9]

It has been demonstrated that economic factors are related to family stress and happiness. Similarly, one could point to the discrepancies between earnings and income potential between husbands and wives, in tracing the feelings of discontent that may pervade their relationship. Social change with respect to a woman's increasing role in the job market may cause a woman to feel resentment if she felt unable to earn a salary commensurate with that of a man, unless she believed that women are unequal, less competent, and therefore deserve a lower salary.[10]

In a study of divorce, Pinard (1966) suggested that marriage and divorce decisions have been increasingly affected by factors outside the micro-world of the family system. Macro-socioeconomic issues were a determinant factor in divorce. Pinard concluded that divorce decisions are dependent upon the larger social systems and their changing forms.[11]

A comparison of census data on different ethnic groups, with respect to intra-familial problems, further underscores the relationship between socioeconomic conditions and family stress. Out-of-wedlock births and abortions are directly related to socioeconomic conditions.[12] Statistics on children's health and mortality rates are directly tied into socioeconomic factors.[13]

Education, a primary factor in determining future economic and social class status, is also directly related to the socioeconomic structure of family life.[14] Conditions in many families have become so critical that many children no longer live at home. To a great extent these conditions reflect the state of the family's economic plight, and the ensuing intra-familial problems which directly result.[15] One of the serious issues of the state of the family is that depicting children as victims of child abuse. Needless to say, class status and economic security alone do not preclude the myriad psychological and social problems of family life. Recent research in child abuse points to the "classless" nature of this phenomenon. If there is a link between socioeconomic factors and the ratio of child abuse, statistics should bear this out.[16]

While statistics and other research data reflect some of the difficulties city life offers its inhabitants, our focus herein is the issues which tie together the state of the family and the state of the social system affecting it. Most importantly, the intersystemic relationship between the family and the larger social institutions points the way toward identifying those forces which intensify the struggle of a family to such a degree that severe behavioral dysfunctioning results. The scope of this book concerns the field of family therapy; therefore, the writer will confine the examination of this issue to the development of psycho-pathological symptoms. These symptoms will be viewed as a response to socio-political forces brought to bear upon the family system and the individual.

Social Pressure and Psychiatric Symptoms

Spiegel (1971) presents a case study of the Tondises, a "sick family." Spiegel found that the isolation which Mrs. Tondis experienced concurrent with her nuclear family departing from the extended family neighborhood evoked a crisis in her nuclear unit. Family treatment ameliorated her condition by forcing the Tondis family to reexamine their assumptions and dissolving their myths about the family. It would seem that treatment provided a way for this family to escape from their prior powerful cultural pressures.

Many investigators have explored the impact of cultural factors on family functioning. Rogelio Diaz Guerrero (1955) explored the etiology of neuroses in the Mexican family. He views neuroses as arising from the imposition of cultural values upon the family system. Wilner, Walkley, Schram, Pinkerton, and Tayback (1960) studied the effects of housing as an environmental factor in mental health. They found some improvement on psychological state variables as a result of an "upward move" in improved housing among a control group of families. Another study relating social factors to mental health was researched by Howells (1971). Listing a number of "social problems" such as "delinquency, criminality, divorce and child neglect," Howells concluded that despite many social conditions, these problems spring from individual psychopathology, i.e., from the dysfunctioning of the emotional substratum of the individual. Examining what Howells labels "hard-core families" he concludes that they are inherently dysfunctional and "stand out very clearly in a welfare state." As an example of the emotional basis of social problems, Howells presents a list of root causes in the families studied. The following are a few examples from this list:

1. As the mother cannot mix with strangers, she sends her children to do her shopping, which is therefore less economically carried out, with consequent waste of finance.
2. The birth of the children was the result of the mother's emotional need to have a baby from which she could have affection.
3. The mother's agitated state results in continuous smoking, with more spending of money.

Doubtless, each of these symptoms and the others described by the author can be answered by explicating the socioeconomic conditions circumscribing it.[17]

Middle and upper class families also have their share in developing behavioral symptoms as a result of family stress. Many of the symptoms are of a nature similar to those of lower class families, though the precipitants appear, at least on the surface, to be markedly different. For example, while lower class families struggle daily with financial pressures, middle and upper middle class families, constantly striving for social and economic status, also feel the effects of the stress to climb the ladder of upward mobility and remain there. If it is not money *per se* that they are after, it is some other form of institutionalized personal growth. "Panaceas," such as those described in an article by Koch and

Koch (1976) in *Psychology Today*,[18] which cited the number of Americans signing up for programs to enrich their marriages, reflect this pressure.

Since many of these families have achieved their economic goals, different pressures resulting from social changes shape new goals and intentions. Ferree (1976) and Travis (1976) cite the serious problems women, and in turn their families, endure—the isolation wives feel all day with their husbands and children away from the home. Broken marriages are but one of the price tags, while the ingestion of drugs for pepping up and others to calm down lead to a variety of addictions and other related problems. Affluent families were studied by Bratter (1975) where inordinate leisure time and participation in a myriad of country clubs, social clubs, and professional committees contributed to many family problems, not the least of which was drug abuse in the adolescent population. As the author points out, in these families the "illusion of being cohesive and harmonious" is more effectively maintained than in impoverished families, where each problem tends to magnify in scope.

The interrelationship between the family and the social system is reflected in the extent to which families of varying background and social position share the common experience of stress. Under the influence of changing social forms and the expectations which evolve from upward mobility, rich and poor alike are not immune from the pervasive force of cultural strains. While many individuals and families choose to work out their problems on their own, many others are forced, either because of the severity of their problems or under the pressure of social institutions, to seek professional help. These individuals frequently enter individual and/or family therapy. The myriad problems affecting families, which are an outgrowth of social forces, are the subject of this paper. Therefore, the focus of the next chapter is on the treatment modality of family therapy.

2. Family Therapy and Consciousness Raising Perspectives on Theories of Change

FAMILY THERAPY

Theoretical Perspectives

Initially, family therapy was an outgrowth of psychoanalytic theory; analytic principles were applied to the family unit with few modifications.[1]

Ackerman (1966), a pioneer in developing a model for family therapy, describes it as:

a special method for treatment of emotional disorders. . . . It is the therapy of a natural living unit; the sphere of therapeutic intervention is not a single individual but the whole family. The therapeutic interview includes all those persons who share the identity of the family and whose behavior is influenced by a circular interchange of emotion within the group. Family psychotherapy, therefore, is a specific method of assessing and intervening upon the family unit as an organismic whole, a way of evaluating family development and adaptation, delineating the distortions of interractional patterns, defining the interplay between interpersonal and intrapersonal conflict and coping, and assessing the relations between the psychosocial functioning of the family group and the emotional destiny of any one member. (p. 209)

This model of therapy presupposed that, "the matrix of human relationships, whether healthy or sick, is the family." The determination was made to treat the individual using the family as the "natural point for intervention." The family model of therapy, at least in the

13

early stages, maintained an allegiance to traditional psychoanalytic
theory as it provided a framework for understanding disturbed behavior.[2] The thrust of therapy was, according to Eisenstein (1956), to
expose "the neurotic components in the constant interplay of mutual
hostility, i.e. in the compulsion to repeat forgotten infantile situations
in the current relationship." Examination of disturbed behavior was
rooted in an intrapsychic paradigm, and treatment was orientated
toward a working through of historical material within the context of
the family. This model was distinguished from individual psychotherapy in that the focus for intervention was the entire familial
constellation. Communication frequently occurs in interpersonal units
and working directly with the complete unit, rather than restricting
interaction to a segment of the unit, facilitated a modification of the
stressful pattern. It was assumed that the interventions on this level
might provide a more effective means of resolving the stress which was
perpetuated by the system.

The treatment of schizophrenia had a marked influence in shaping
theories of family therapy. Bowen (1960) studied the mother-patient
relationship, concluding that the entire family played a primary role in
its development. Wynne (1958), working at the National Institute of
Mental Health, studied psychosis occurring in late adolescence or early
adulthood with focus on the family's role in the development of
individual identity. Other contributors were Fleck (1960) and Lidz
(1958). Both studied families, and the development of psychosis.[3] The
influence of psychoanalysis is apparent, even for family therapists who
have moved well beyond traditional models of treatment (Bowen,
1961; Framo, 1962; Whitaker, 1958). Bowen's conceptual model
emphasized issues of attachment and separation inside the family
system. A primary aim of the therapeutic intervention was toward
helping individual members achieve "differentiation of self."

In working with families Bowen observed the myriad ways in which
family members are emotionally "stuck" to one another and how
difficult it is for some individuals to separate themselves from other
members of the family.

Bowen began working with the entire family constellation, but soon
narrowed his focus to include the identified patient (often a child) and
the parent subsystem. This triad was the precursor leading to the
concept of "triangles" consisting of therapeutic work with units of three
individuals. It is Bowen's contention that separation is best achieved
through this model because the therapist (who is separate from the

triad) could aid in differentiating the identity of each member from the other.

Bowen theorized that the emotional attachment each spouse has to the other duplicates the relationship each spouse had to his/her own family of origin. From this perspective, attention to cross-generational relationships grew in importance. While for some family therapists cross-generational issues were explored with the spouse-subsystem, for others, like Carl Whitaker, the extended kin were invited to join the process—at least for a few prechosen sessions. In this setting, it is common to find three generations of kin, all involved in therapy. Noting the magnitude of the therapeutic task, Whitaker prefers to work in the presence of a cotherapist who, he contends, acts as a mainstay or sounding board for him. Actually it is common to overhear both therapists engaging each other as the rest of the family looks on.

Considered somewhat of a maverick by traditional standards, Whitaker eschews therapy that is rigidly tied to an inflexible therapeutic model. As a result of this attitude, Whitaker's therapeutic style is so highly personalized that few protégés can copy it successfully.

Whitaker is expressedly antitechnique when technique is utilized instead of an authentic encounter. Indeed, he introduces an element of freedom into the therapeutic setting that departs rather sharply from more traditional models of treatment.

The increasing size of the group in therapy is expounded most dramatically in the work of Ross Speck. Collaborating with Carolyn Attneave, they assemble, at least for one or two sessions, not only all extended kin of the identified patient, but also friends, relatives, and just about anyone who has had something to do with this patient. As many as twenty or more people gather in the home of the family in therapy—a meeting modeled very much like a tribal assemblage where group healing is practiced. Instead of long-term therapy, this model is designed to explore new connections and resources for the troubled person and his/her family. Needless to say, the experience of being surrounded by so many caring people is an emotional event of some intensity and drama.

Clearly, a model such as the one just described sets itself apart from more traditional psychotherapy models; this is so, not only because of the size of the group, but also because of the increasing deemphasis upon intrapsychic structure as a means to remedy dysfunctional behavior and conflict. Therapy conducted without focusing upon an intrapsychic model not only produced variations in treatment methodology but more, it excited new speculation concerning the etiology of symptoms.

A growing number of family therapists responded to observations made during treatment that dysfunctional behavior was not necessarily due to intrapsychic forces at all, but rather to problems in communication patterns. Questioning the basis of the medical model and its reliance on psychoanalytic theory for the treatment of dysfunctional behavior, Haley (1963) began to explore symptomatic behavior as "a way of dealing with another person." This approach shifted the study of behavior from an individual to a communication system. While traditional family therapy was also involved in treating the individual through a system, the shift to communications had broader implications. The most far-reaching was that the earlier conceptualizations of behavior had been constructed upon a false paradigm; that behavior was not a function of intrapsychic forces but rather a direct result of human communication.[4] Jackson (1957), Minuchin (1974), Ruesch (1949), and a host of other family therapists moved away from the traditional intrapsychic paradigm, developing a number of new treatment innovations which departed from the earlier models used in family therapy.[5]

Traditional diagnostic categories which were used to describe individual psychopathology were replaced by terms which described relationships in process. Models of family process were conceptualized through many frameworks such as cybernetics, mathematics, and information theory.

Watzlawick, Weakland, and Fisch (1974) studied the structure of changing behavior by analyzing the properties of change within a system. They explicated two different types of change that could occur: the first is change that occurs within a given system in which the system itself remains unchanged; the second is change that alters the structure of the system itself. Utilizing concepts from cybernetics, communication and change were understood to express the properties of a feedback system and to this a therapeutic intervention required an interruption of chronic feedback circles which maintain dysfunctional behavior.

This approach to problem solving is a pragmatic one, and insight, traditionally believed to be a precursor for change, is devalued. Instead, attention is focused upon which behaviors are maintaining a problem and how these behaviors block problem resolution. To this the therapeutic task is to formulate a strategy that will interdict (block) a chronic pattern, thus forcing a change in the social network. Once the therapist can discern and implement this strategy, family members can no longer continue behaving toward one another in a way that maintains the problem behavior.

A further notion belonging to this communication paradigm is that in many cases it is the approach utilized to solve a problem that becomes the problem itself. In other words, not every issue in a relationship can or should be resolved; in fact, the idea that all problems in a family yield to resolution if only the appropriate method can be found is itself a misconception. To this it was posited that often working to solve a problem may perpetuate and/or exacerbate it.

This work led to the study of the structure of communication, and since symptoms are communicative they are studied as part of a social context.

Treatment in context has been undertaken in the study of psychosomatic illness in which Minuchin, Rosman, and Baker (1978) carried out research on anorexia nervosa. After extensive observations, these therapists shifted away from the medical model of pathology and began treating psychologically related medical conditions in a family context.

The evolving viewpoint is that the family system is directly involved in the exacerbation of many physical conditions, and treatment must include a transactional analysis of family interaction.

To Minuchin, symptoms serve as a regulator in the family system. Melding concepts from Bowen's work on "family triangles" with communication theory, Minuchin and his cohorts observed that psychosomatic symptoms serve the family by maintaining familiar patterns of behavior. In fact, it was noticed that the growth of one or more family members inevitably produced tension and disequilibrium in the family unit.

A key concept introduced by Minuchin and discussed in more detail further on in this book is the process of "joining" a family. Minuchin believes that a successful intervention requires the therapist to join the field of stabilized family interventions in order to observe and change them. Mindful of the power of the system, he is convinced that the therapist can exert force and challenge that power only from inside the family system. The concept which refers to the self-regulatory principle inside a family system is homeostasis.

Homeostasis as a family system concept is attributed to the work of Don Jackson, a psychiatrist interested in human communications who was associated with the Mental Research Institute in Palo Alto. His observations of family process led to a discernment that a family engages in a continuous interplay of dynamic interventions that move toward the maintenance of an equilibrium of patterns among family members. Echoing a similar concern, Minuchin (1974) states that, "within this system are universal rules governing family organization," and that, "the origin of these expectations is buried in years of explicit and implicit negotiations among family members, often around small daily events." (p. 52.)

In his most recent work, Minuchin enlarges his systems paradigm to include the ideas that people form part of "field structures." Here, he is showing a concern with more than the interactions inside a family system and includes observations of how the social system constrains and governs a family in transaction with it. Models of family therapy have extended the study of the family system to influences which go beyond the boundary separating the family as a subsystem from larger social systems.

In related studies, the examination of socio-cultural patterns was brought to bear upon the understanding of family behavior and social change. Spiegel (1971) concentrated upon the family as a subsystem of society. Influenced by the writings of Whitehead, Spiegel sought to understand process in a space-time dimension.[7] His model was one in which each subsystem could be understood as a "function of transformation processes which fit together the systems so that they achieve an equilibrium in which each facilitates the operations of the other." Spiegel, concerned with cultural values, social roles, and psychodynamics, concluded that behavior could best be understood if one takes into account cultural, organizational, and individual determinants. "The principal merit of this approach," writes Spiegel, "is that it permits us to detect the connection between cultural strain, family conflict, and individual pathology." (p. 198.)

Spiegel developed a systems model in which the nature of the pathological process in the family was understood as primarily a problem of role conflict which disturbed the harmonious functioning of the family as a social organization.[8] In various case presentations, Spiegel depicts the struggle which ensues when family background is at odds with the prevailing socio-cultural values orientations.[9]

He was influenced in his writings by Florence Kluckhohn, a social anthropologist. From her research, Spiegel developed a concern for cultural issues that he believed necessary to study in order to analyze and treat family problems. It was Spiegel's impression that the family as a subsystem occupies a class position in the larger social field that either fits or is in tension with other social systems in that field (community).

A major aspect of Spiegel's work concerns the understanding of role theory. Explicating role theory from sociology to developing models for family therapy, Spiegel reached beyond the family subsystem and examined data from a cross-disciplinary perspective. He argues that role analysis provides a method for conceptualizing behavior inside a family as the family transacts with larger social forms. In role theory, a role represents a socially regulated way of responding to the instinctual needs of an individual—whether that individual is observed as a member of a family or a member of any other social unit.

For a therapist, the task is to study and discern the appropriateness or adequacy through which a social role appears to satisfy personal and system needs. In other words, it is important to clarify just how well role behavior organizes experience toward personal satisfaction.

Spiegel did not narrow his focus solely to role analysis but added that in order to complete an understanding of family dynamics, an investigation must include attention to the family value system. As such, this embraces areas which include the structure of moral standards, mores, patterns of motivation, and interpersonal relations.

A similar conceptualization of family process translated into treatment intervention is described in the work of Auerswald (1968). Using a systems approach labeled "ecological," he puts forward the idea that family therapy "can be brought to arenas much larger than the therapy room or even the home." (p. 313.) In a related case history, Auerswald described the mobilization of an interdisciplinary team in the community to treat a runaway girl. Breaking with traditional forms, Auerswald challenged the fragmentation of mental health services into segments and raised the question, referring to the case of the runaway, "as to which system deserves the prefix, schizo." Although Auerswald is not the first family therapist to break with the mainstream in the delivery of services, he is one of a small group who (a) broke with conventional services and (b) questioned where the label "schizo" is appropriately placed—suggesting that it may belong on subsystems outside the family unit.

The evolution of change in theoretical assumptions, coupled with a growing acceptance of an enlarged target for treatment (the notion that the family unit, rather than the individual, was the "patient"), made possible new forms of intervention.

However, despite the shift in theoretical perspective, and the steady growth of what were considered to be radical methods of therapy, the thrust of treatment continued to emphasize repair and reconstruction of the family unit. To this extent "radical" changes in treatment within the discipline of therapy were still "radical" in name only, insofar as the family as a subsystem was to fit and adapt into the larger social system.[10]

FAMILY THERAPY

Treatment Perspectives

In treating the nuclear family, the thrust of family therapy is to "produce a harmonious, healthy, adjusted family."[11] (Howells, 1971, p. 57.) "In family psychiatry," writes Howells, "the goal is a healthy family, with of course, healthy individuals, a task always limited by the fact that social ill health pulls the family towards conformity to its norms." (p. 60.) Acknowledging that there are forces in society which promote "ill-health," Howells points out that in clinical practice the sick family is the best vantage point from which to work, though attention to social influence must be considered. The perspective from which these social ills are considered is published in a separate article written by Howells (1966). While he lists a number of social ills which negatively affect a family, Howells concludes that these social ills evolve from "individual psychopathology, i.e., from the dysfunctioning of the emotional substratum of the individual."[12] Needless to say, the thrust is towards treating the emotionally ill family, to enable them to overcome their condition and function more effectively in the community.

It would be easy to reason that Howells, with his psychiatric training, represents the more conservative and traditional element of family therapy; however, the situation is not substantially different in less orthodox circles. Haley (1976) calls attention to his clients' social context. He recognizes the impracticality of becoming a social revolutionary when dealing with a client and attends instead to the social unit he can change—the family. Haley, a problem-solving strategist in family therapy, writes:

The task for the therapist has no easy solution. Whatever radical position he takes as a citizen, his obligation as a therapist is to define the social unit that can change, to solve the presenting problem of a client. To war with mental hospitals, courts and welfare agencies does not usually achieve the goal of therapy, although sometimes it may be necessary. The effectiveness of the therapist is evaluated in terms of the outcome of his therapy, not in terms of the moral stance he takes on, his justifiable indignation at the society that is contributing to the problems he is trying to solve. The most useful point of view for the therapist is the idea that there is sufficient variety in any situation, so that some better arrangement can be made.[13] (p.5)

Minuchin (1974) developed structural family therapy, a method which also departed from more traditional clinical models. The social context is considered of great importance in Minuchin's conceptualizations of family dysfunction. Present-centered in his approach, Minuchin targets his methods on changing family organizations based upon a belief that the normal difficulties of family life transcend cultural differences. As a social unit, Minuchin concerns himself with the difficulties families have in successfully managing their passage along socially determined developmental tasks. He too recognizes the family as a subsystem of the larger social field, but, methodologically, works for a more harmonious adjustment—inside the family. He deals with the family as a subsystem transacting with larger social forms.[5]

In his latest book coauthored with Rosman and Baker, Minuchin (1978) reemphasizes the importance of the systems model as a framework for the diagnosis and treatment of anorexia nervosa—a disturbance characterized by severe appetite and weight loss generally seen in female adolescents.

The systems model developed by Minuchin for the treatment of psychosomatic illness is presented as follows:

Extrafamilial stress   Family organization and functioning

Vulnerable child   Symptomatic child

Physiological endocrine and biochemical mediating mechanisms

To treat the anorectic patient, Minuchin observes that not eating is controlled and affected by the way in which the parents of the patient interact to influence a resumption of eating. From this observation, a

treatment strategy to change the patient's appetite and willingness to
eat required a change in the interactional patterns of the family system.
While Minuchin does not discard important data derived from medical
and psychological analysis, his perspective includes attention to transactional relations between a number of system variables.

Minuchin formulates his therapeutic goals to include a reduction of
symptoms (no small matter in cases such as anorexia nervosa) and a
provision for the family to enlarge upon their patterns of interaction so
that a better adaptation can be made to the social field.

While it can be argued that these goals, should they be achieved,
represent the best family therapy has to offer, it can also be argued that
an adjustment to the social field would not in itself represent a
successful therapeutic outcome.

We can look at anorexia nervosa as a case in point. Indeed, there are
processes inside the family system which may be responsible for
inducing and maintaining this life-threatening condition. Minuchin
identifies one element as "enmeshment," an overinvolvement of parent
with child, where differences are obscured in order to gain a mutual
accommodation between them. Added to this, the anoretic family
places a high premium on tightening the boundaries that keep family
members involved with each other and apart from outside contact and
influence. An exaggerated emphasis on bodily functions completes the
family picture.

But this is not the whole story. If the treatment model is true to the
systems concept, then the therapist is compelled to study the social
field. What Minuchin fails to do is to position the anoretic family in the
social field and examine how an excessive preoccupation with "thin-
ness" and dieting, manipulated by the fashion industry, influences
many women to crave designer clothes that for many require an
inexorable commitment to weight loss. It was only a few years ago that
Twiggy was recognized as the foremost fashion model in England and
in the United States. A worshipping of the body, controlled and
manipulated by advertising and the media, may also be a factor in
fostering conditions such as anorexia nervosa.

America in the 1970s has been referred to as the Culture of
Narcissism by Christopher Lasch, social critic and professor of History
at the University of Rochester. Adjustment to the fashion industry and
other social forms may be an uneasy peace for a family to attain. Such
an adjustment does little to liberate individuals from socially induced

behaviors, though indeed they might improve their relationships—at least for a while.

But what is the alternative? To answer this it is necessary to look first at some of the writings which critique models of therapy and then advance the understanding of systems theory to develop methodologies which incorporate an examination of the social field directly into family process.

There has been a good deal of writing from the field of mental health in which arguments have been put forth severely criticizing the movement for failing to deal with the social aspects of behavioral disorders. One of its most severe critics has been Thomas Szasz (1970). He writes:

While I maintain that mental illnesses do not exist, I obviously do not imply or mean that the social and psychological occurrences to which this label is attached also do not exist. Like the personal and social troubles that people had in the Middle Ages, contemporary human problems are real enough. It is the labels we give them that concern me, and having labeled them, what we do about them.[14] The demonological concept of problems in living gave rise to therapy along theological lines. Today, a belief in mental illness implies—nay, requires therapy along medical or psychotherapeutic lines. (p. 21)

Szasz's arguments were not aimed at the failure of therapy to deal with social influences, but rather of therapy itself as ideologically bound into the social structure—and to this extent, serving as an agent of the state.[15] Questioning the relationship between mental health and social adaptation, Szasz writes:

In the past and still today in some societies, adaptation to society has tended to be highly valued . . . as a sign of mental health; and failure to adapt has been even more strongly regarded as a sign of mental health. . . . There are occasions and situations in which, from the point of view of mental health, rebellion and non-conformity may be far more important than social adaptation. But no criteria are given for distinguishing, "from the point of view of mental health," the situations to which we ought to conform from those against which we ought to rebel. (p. 3)

While Szasz has gained a reputation as a severe critic of traditional therapy for its failure to deal with the political aspects of mental health, other critics have assumed a more radical posture.

Writing in *The Radical Therapist,* Richard Kunnes, M. D. has this to say about therapy: "When you do 'therapy' always suggest various political settings to help 'patients' deal with their alienation and oppression. Always attempt to help patients understand the political causes of their symptoms." (p. 31.) In the same book a more radical pronouncement is expressed by Claude Steiner: "Paranoia is a state of heightened awareness. Most people are persecuted beyond their wildest delusions. Those who feel at ease are insensitive. Depression is the result of alienation of human to human. Violent anger is a healthy reaction to oppression. Drug abuse is taught to children by their alcoholic, nicotinic, aspirinic elders." (p. 282.)

For Anne Kent Rush, author of *Feminism As Therapy,* therapy is "synonymous with socialization, that is adjustment to the current cultural mode."

Dennis Jaffe, writing in the *Journal of Humanistic Psychology,* attacks traditional therapy for its commitment to "promote the general welfare by setting standards of morality through diagnosis of what a healthy person is and exerting control on the boundary when people stray from such a standard. Thus they emphasize limits and proper behavior rather than self-determination and creative expression." (p. 26.)

Certainly family therapy has not encouraged rebellion or liberation from social constraints beyond which rebellion is envisioned as a conditional aspect of normal developmental stages of growth. Nor did it develop theories of change based upon the effects of socio-political forces upon individual personality and/or family life.

WOMEN'S STUDIES AND CONSCIOUSNESS

Theoretical Perspectives

To identify a theory of change which placed its primary emphasis upon understanding the socio-political structure as a determiner or shaper of human consciousness, the writer turns to the women's movement and to the theory of consciousness-raising.[16]

Since the nuclear family occupies a central role in this thesis, it is the family understood through the women's movement and consciousness-raising that will be explored. While the women's movement is a pluralistic one, feminist writers who have assumed a particularly strong posture against the nuclear family might be considered as representing a more radical segment. The family receives a radically different assessment from this perspective than from that which has heretofore been written in family therapy publications. The work of Rowbotham (1974) elucidates this clearly.

The condition of the preservation of the "ideal" family as of the "ideal" fuck are definitions of female nature which are not only imposed, but imposed in order to maintain the interest men have in finding compensation from their exploitation and alienation capitalism forces on them at work. Continuance of this situation produces not only a distorted reality in the family and a continual source of aggression and resentment as human beings fail to live up to their impossible stereotypes of one another, it allows the values of commodity production to mold and determine aspects of human experience which are apparently completely separate from work. (p. 53)

The author suggests that sexuality serves as a safety valve while "men and women devour their children, regarding them as property; they use their 'love' as blackmail, care becomes an investment." (p. 53)

Women and children as dependent, helpless property is treated in the writing of Firestone (1970). Indicting the nuclear family for its repressive forms, the author identifies male/female polarities shaped by cultural myth:

The mother is expected to love the child devotedly, even unconditionally, whereas the father, on the other hand, seldom takes an active interest in infants—certainly not in their intimate care—and later, when the son is older, loves him conditionally, in response to performance and achievement. (p. 49)

According to Firestone, these issues are deeply embedded in political ideology and require a thorough analysis.

Though the sex class system may have originated in fundamental biological conditions, this does not guarantee once the biological basis of oppression has been swept away that women and children will be freed. On the contrary, the new technology, especially fertility control, may be used against them [women] to reinforce the entrenched system of exploitation. (p. 10)

Chesler has compared the common experience of women in both marriage and psychotherapy (1971). Traditional psychotherapy and marriage, according to Chesler in an article in *The Radical Therapist* (1971),

both isolate women from each other; both institutions emphasize individual rather than or before collective solutions to a woman's problem. Both institutions may be viewed as redramatizations of a little girl's relation to her father in a male dominated society. Both institutions are based on a woman's helplessness and dependence on a "stronger" male or female authority figure— as husband or psychotherapist. (p. 176) [17]

Few writers have been as harsh on the nature of the family as Reich (1949). It was his contention that the family's political function is to "cripple people sexually, and create individuals who fear life and authority." In any patriarchal society, Reich believed that the family is the keystone for the social order, and that sexual repression is the mode through which the maintenance of the state is possible. In 1915, Goodsell described the normal family.

It is interesting to juxtapose this definition with that of Reich. Goodsell writes:

America contains countless homes where true affection and mutual attraction have bound families together in the strongest of human bonds. Such homes furnish cogent reasons for believing in the future of wholesome and happy family life. . . . On the trouble in family life, until one standard of personal purity be held up for both sexes, until absolute monogamy may be the ideal held before our youth from boyhood, this evil, with its disintegrating effect upon family life, will not disappear from among us. . . . It remains true that the wife and grown daughters have frequently failed to recognize their responsibility for the maintenance of the home. (p. 477)

Similar conceptions of home life and women's place in it are precisely what have inspired women to rise up in anger and resentment. Greer (1970) challenges the male dominant myth, writing that,

the patrilineal family depends upon the free gift by women of the right of paternity to men. Paternity is not an intrinsic relationship: it cannot be proved, except negatively. The most intense vigilance will not insure absolutely that any man is the father of his son. (p. 217)

Historically, the division of humanity by sex roles, class, and occupation has indeed been important to the maintenance of the social structure. Janeway (1972) gives credence to this but argues that, "as long as sheer physical strength had a meaningful premium attached to it," there was some reality. However, the fact that these conditions no longer exist challenges the forces which continue to support them.[18]

The evolving issue from the women's movement was that the structure of the family is not a natural condition but is rather a response to social influence and change. It was a short step for women to begin raising issues concerning child raising, and more, the state of childhood itself. Since so much of a woman's role in the family was intertwined in child bearing and child raising functions, it was clear that new definitions of this relationship were required. Aries (1975) studied the historical development of childhood, citing that affection was merely a by-product of family life. In his view, myths concerning the sanctity of parent-child love developed as a contemporary phenomenon. Such research provided strong arguments for antifamily polemicists. According to Firestone (1970), in the Middle Ages there was no such thing as childhood. It was sometime "after the fourteenth century, with the development of the bourgeoisie and empirical science, this situation slowly began to evolve."[19] As childhood became a delineated period in the life span, it required special attitudes and behaviors as a result. Not only did this development affect the nature of the family, but "new concepts about the life cycle in our society are organized around institutions, e.g. adolescence, a construction of the nineteenth century, was built to facilitate conscription for military service. The development of the schools, and later compulsory education followed suit."[20] This added the pressure for parents, not only to make certain that their children attended school and achieved, but also patterned their behavior to fit that which the school required in order to succeed.[21]

In effect, social change and the evolving pattern of family life linked both women and children together as subjugated victims both in the family and the society. Firestone (1970) summarized this view:

Women and children were now in the same lousy boat and their oppressions began to reinforce one another. To the mystique and glories of childbirth, the grandeur of "natural" female creativity, was now added a new mystique about the glories of childhood itself and the "creativity" of childrearing. (Why, my dear, what could be more creative than raising a child?) By now people have forgotten what history has proven—that raising a child is tantamount to retarding his development. The best way to raise a child is to lay off. (p. 91)

The issues raised were political in scope. It was not simply that stress and strain in family life were a response to the imperatives inside the family system, but rather that the nature and form of the family itself was brought into question. The myths which in the past supported the nuclear family as a model of potential growth and deep satisfaction were challenged. Women were becoming sharply aware of the limitations and pressures brought to bear on their lives as a direct effect of maintaining their socially determined roles as wives, mothers, and houseservants.

Families in stress often turn to professionally trained people, such as family therapists, to help solve their problems. However, a growing number of women seek help from their peers in nonprofessional settings. Many of these women, recognizing the political nature of their stress, choose to avoid conventional treatment and embark upon new roads to examine the possibilities of personal liberation. One of these endeavors was the formation of women's consciousness-raising groups.

Consciousness Raising—Perspectives on the Process of Change

There is a difference between identifying the issues that have led to stress, dissatisfaction, and oppression, and changing one's situation as a result of understanding and awareness. While it may be necessary to first discern that which one chooses to change, the process through which change occurs is a distinct and separate experience.

To begin to understand the nature of consciousness raising, it is helpful to draw a comparison between this mode of change and that which would ordinarily result from traditional forms of psychotherapy. Steiner (1971) is helpful in delineating this distinction. He begins by offering the following case example:

There is the woman who, angered by her husband's domination, ceases to enjoy sex with him . . . if she fails to recognize her oppression, she will conclude that she is at fault; that she is "frigid." While if she becomes aware of the source of her anger, she will recognize that her loving nature is intact.

This means that the difference between alienation and anger about one's oppression is unawareness of deception. "Psychiatry," according to Steiner, "has a great deal to do with the deception of human beings about their oppression."

Oppression + Deception = Alienation

Oppression + Awareness = Anger

and finally,

Liberation = Awareness + Contact

The awareness Steiner refers to is the identification of oppressive sources, an identification which leads to anger. From there, this anger, in order not to become undifferentiated or neurotic, must be translated into "contact"—a term which signifies "contact with other human beings who, united, will move against the oppression." (p. 6.) This is a key, for it is in the group experience that contact is possible. Steiner underscores that, "neither awareness by itself nor contact by itself will produce liberation. It is the banding together which results in liberation." Gornick (1971) defines the process of consciousness-raising this way:

Consciousness-raising is the name given to the feminist practice of examining one's personal experience in the light of sexism; i.e. that theory which explains woman's subordinate position in society as a result of a cultural decision to confer direct power on men and only indirect power on women. . . . Coming together, as they do, week after week for many months, the women who are in a group begin to exchange an extraordinary sense of multiple identification that is encouraged by the technique's instruction to look for explanations for each part of one's history in terms of the social or cultural dynamics created by sexism—rather than in terms of the personal dynamic, as one would do in a psychotherapist's group session.

Finally, Gornick adds, "it is looking at one's history and experience—something like shaking a kaleidoscope and watching all the same pieces rearrange themselves into an altogether other picture—one that suddenly makes the color and the shape of each piece appear startling new and alive and full of meaning." [22]

Sarachild (1971) explains the consciousness-raising experience in this way.

We always stay in touch with our feelings. We assume that our feelings are telling us something from which we can learn . . . that our feelings mean something worth analyzing . . . that our feelings are saying something political, something reflecting fear that something bad will happen to us or hope, desire, knowledge that something good will happen to us.

The author explains that feelings were always available to women and that from this vantage point, being in touch has been an asset. It is how the translation of these feelings into action such as hysteria, whining, bitching, that was the problem, for in the translations, there was an absence of political awareness. Hanisch (1971) calls the women's

consciousness-raising group experience, "a political therapy" rather
than personal therapy. Chesler (1971) further clarifies the distinction
between personal psychotherapy, at least from the woman's standpoint, versus the consciousness-raising experience. She writes:

> For most women, the psychotherapeutic encounter is just one more instance of
> an unequal relationship, just one more instance of a power relationship in
> which she is submissive and the authority figure is dominant. I wonder how well
> such a structure can encourage independence—or healthy dependence—in a
> woman? (p. 179)

Finally, writes Chesler, "Both psychotherapy and marriage may be
viewed as a way of socially controlling and oppressing women." Her
explanation of how this occurs is that in psychotherapy and in marriage,
"a woman can safely express (and politically defuse) her anger and
unhappiness—by experiencing them as a form of emotional illness."

Similar observations have been cited from men's liberation and
consciousness-raising groups. Farrell (1974) draws a distinction between traditional psychotherapy and consciousness-raising groups from
a masculine perspective. According to Farrell, men often become
involved in consciousness-raising groups only after learning to communicate in therapy.[23] In men's groups the support is focused upon
illumination of "how anxieties about powerlessness, combined with
expectations for power, make us [men] fight to be in control."
Comparing marriage counseling to consciousness-raising groups, Farrell writes:

> In marriage counseling, couples feel they have a unique problem which only an
> experienced counselor and large outlays of money can solve. In consciousness-
> raising groups, problems are seen as almost inevitable given the way both sexes
> have been socialized. For many couples, consciousness-raising is more suppor-
> tive because of the challenge it gives the couple to overcome the culture, rather
> than fight each other.

Nichols (1975), writing from a men's perspective, says, "Thus the
liberation of each man from power complexes begins as a personal
liberation." He too acknowledges that liberation involves a political
analysis of power, and that men, from their particular perspective, are
indeed victims, perhaps as much as are women—though the issues of
power itself are translated into counterpointed forms.[24]

Looking at these issues from a systems point of view, it seems clear that women's and children's liberation is intertwined with the liberation of men. While it is true that both men and women can work toward their own personal liberation, there are issues which are inextricably rooted in the relationship between them. Some women and some men choose the vehicle of consciousness-raising groups in order to increase their personal liberation. At times, these groups are mixed and avail both men and women of the opportunity to work on common issues together. But many men and women do not take this route— particularly those who struggle in conventional marriages. While their struggles are also political, and often involve children as well, they choose to resolve their problems through conventional forms of psychotherapy and family counseling. In these marriages the issues are often intensified, for the emotional bonding in marriages not only tends to blur the political nature of the struggle, but exacerbates its volatility. In the conventional marriage, the politic of the social order is dramatized as a social subsystem required to maintain socio-political forms in order to maintain itself. While therapy is often successful in alleviating the pain, it does little to alter the relationship between the political issues and the ensuing struggle of the family as a collective social unit to survive. With this problem, the writer turns to the possibility of including socio-political consciousness-raising in family therapy.

3. Socio-Political Consciousness Raising In Family Therapy

Theoretical Perspectives

Consciousness-raising in family therapy presents a theoretical paradox. While consciousness-raising is concerned primarily with liberating the individual, family therapy is traditionally concerned with conserving the integrity of the family unit. Families in stress, applying for family therapy services, anticipate a relief from their problems and a corollary outcome of functioning more effectively as a unit. They expect that the therapist who works with them intends to strengthen their relationships along the conventional model, characteristic of the nuclear family. A study by Laws (1971) corroborates that the families' expectations are well-founded in this regard. He concluded in his research that the majority of marital counselors far and away favored an adjustment to the structure of a traditional marriage as a treatment objective. Since men are generally presumed to be at the head of the family, both in the nuclear unit and in social organizations, it is also conceivable that families would expect to be treated by a male therapist. Chesler (1971) analyzed the records of middle class clinic populations and discovered that the families preferred male to female therapists on a two to one margin.

Social change has to some extent influenced the perceptions of family members around male/female issues. Similar changes have occurred within the field of therapy. Rice and Rice (1977) have remodeled their approach to marital counseling by responding to the changes in women's behavior and the literature coming out of the women's momement. Evaluating the problems intrinsic to traditional sex role stereotypes in contemporary marriages, the authors introduce "non-sexist marital therapy" into the treatment arena. Here social issues of a

33

theoretical nature are translated into techniques in order to restructure "marital patterning." (p. 26.)

Wesley (1975), a clinical social worker similarly sensitive to issues of sex-role stereotyping, recommends consciousness-raising for women. Taking a balanced approach, she focuses treatment toward the liberation of the woman from the sex-role constraints and then elicits support from the family to cope with and integrate these changes. It is the woman who is understood to be in the pivotal role as the family system changes in response to her new role definitions. Within this process pressure is brought to bear upon each family member to examine and expand sex-role patterns. From this perspective liberation is defined as a change in role function. There is an expansion of the behavior options available to women and subsequently the strain in family living is reduced.

On the other end of the spectrum, consciousness-raising is a process dedicated to liberation. Mander and Rush (1974) describe their work with feminism as a therapy in which personal issues assume a political context. In their work, change does not mean agreeing to an expanded definition of sex-role responsibility within a couple, but rather an exploration of the personal and political sources of pain. As an example, the authors write,

a woman continually blames herself for her inadequacies, let us say, the group works with her to explore what part is her responsibility and what part is imposed upon her by society. Thus she is encouraged to assume responsibility and to relinquish responsibility at the same time for that part that is not hers so that she can be freed of that burden and grow. (p. 17)

Critics of consciousness-raising only for women voice their objections on theoretical grounds. Barber (1975) criticizes women's liberation as a one-sided affair, contending that liberation must involve everyone, though he agrees that the issues raised by women are valid. It is his contention that a distinction must be made "between oppression as a particular kind of relationship, than as a feature of relationships in general; namely, a relationship which is intrinsically and consciously exploitative." (p. 32.)

Barber explains the relationship between women and men not as intrinsically exploitive or oppressive, but rather "at the level of nature, hormonal differentiation, sexual magnetism and the requisites of heterosexual production; and at the level of culture, childrearing, companionship and love." (p. 34.) Translating this into the family, Barber writes, "in our heterosexuality lies the last hopes for mutualism; when the family is perceived as but one more disguise for interest assertion and domination, when the polity is defamilialized and the family politicized, the disintegration of society cannot be far off." (p. 34.)

In contrast, feminist writers have been severe critics of the nuclear family, frequently calling for its destruction (Firestone, 1970; Greer, 1971; Rowbotham, 1971). Mander and Rush (1974) cite the failure of other cultural revolutions to change people's behavior because they did not address "a real structural/emotional alternation at its core," the nuclear family. "Women and children liberation," according to the authors, "is the end of culture and the nuclear family as we know it." (p. 50.) Therapy in its traditional form is chastized for clearly separating therapy and the state. Both authors are convinced that this is a result of the unwillingness of men to be dethroned and lose socioeconomic power. In this regard, "every therapy is teaching you, either overtly or indirectly, some kind of politics in the way that therapy recommends you relate to power." (p. 51.)

The dialectics of power involve issues that have polarized men and women and also joined them together in a similar manner to the dialectic of sex. Liberation, as a dialectical process requires the reconciliation and acceptance of opposites. In this context, dialectic is understood to mean envisioning the world as a process whereby a natural flux of action and reaction of opposites are also inseparable and interpenetrating (Firestone, 1970). Hobbs (1970) discusses the issue of liberation for a woman in marriage. She writes, "this breaking out of the doll's house has as much meaning for the male as for the female. It is the beginning of his liberation." (p. 13.) In another passage, Hobbs describes male liberation in the following way: "It is a fact that this choice of the male (a life-long occupation) is often as not illusory. With all dreams men have, the majority end up planting corn, digging in a mine, driving a truck or shuffling paper, stuck in their places like flies in jam." (p. 14.) Distinguishing this entrapment from a woman's, Hobbs writes:

Yet there is a profound difference between a man's lot and a woman's. If he does not actually have a choice of occupation and a control over the expenditure of his years, he—at least for his growing years—thinks he has and as a child this invests his games and all his contacts with the world with an exploratory element. . . . Because we (women) have not experienced this sense of free destiny, most of us lack the critical growth of imagination that should accompany it. (p. 15)

As a prescription for freedom, Hobbs underscores the dialectical process, writing, "we will know that we are not male and can never be male, that he is not female and can never be female, and this knowledge will bring us freedom." (p. 18.) Barber (1975) further criticizes the women's liberation movement for taking an uncompromising and inaccurate view of liberation, and writes:

The just aim of feminism is the liberation of women from abuse; the liberation of women from womanhood serves that goal only as suicide serves the mitigation of suffering. The goal of personal self-realization is the fulfillment of the potential of women and men as members of the human polity; an abstract emancipation from natural identity that leaves individuals adrift with free-floating, transient characters guaranteed to be as meaningless as they are autonomous serves self-realization not at all. To choose meaningfully, to invest freedom with significance; to root ideals; and to accommodate the guiding dictates of a no longer omnipotent nature with moral standards of an increasingly potent autonomy: these are the real tasks of liberation. (p. 128)

Whether it is the writing of radical feminists, or less severe critics on family life such as Barber and Hobbs, the consensus favors, at the very least, a transformation of the nature of the nuclear family as we know it. In each instance liberation is the primary goal. This raises a key question: can family therapy as a modality dedicated to the conservation of the family liberate people and at the same time conserve the family structure? This salient issue is explored in the following section within the context of a series of theoretical models.

Theoretical Models for Change

The following models for change are presented in order to depict the evolution of systems theory as it pertains to three distinct theoretical frameworks: family therapy, consciousness-raising and women's liberation, and finally, consciousness-raising in family therapy.

The development of these models was influenced by the work of Minuchin (1974) and Spiegel (1971).

Each boundary separating one system from another is differentiated by the following key (Minuchin, 1974, p. 53).

Key to Models
------ permeable boundary
_____ rigid boundary
M—male   F—female   C—children   I—individual

I. TRANSACTIONAL FIELD

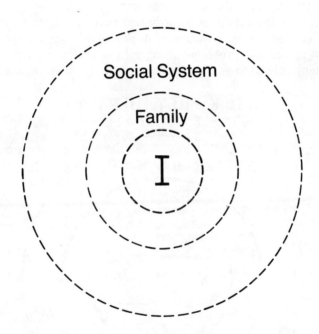

In the transactional field, all systems are interdependent.

No one of its parts could be omitted without destroying the whole field, for all
are conceived as being in a functional relation with all others in an inclusive
system of relationships. It is not that the whole is greater than the sum of its
parts. Rather, the whole is a way of exhibiting the functional relation between
parts. Whole and parts are complementary and indispensable to each other.
(Spiegel, 1971, p. 41).

In the circumscribed area labeled social system one considers

dynamic processes pertaining to knowledge of class status, economic
and occupational systems, education, religious influences, government,
the mass media, and any other large-scale power system impacting
upon family structure.

The area contained within the boundaries of Family refers to
knowledge of the structure of the family-kinship system. Here the focus
rests with discerning family relations, values, myths, the assignment of
culturally defined roles, and an assessment of interactive behavior
between family members. An analysis of the family system is formu-
lated in accord with a therapist's theoretical framework.

Finally, the Individual as a subsystem pertains to the structure of
knowledge concerning psychological processes such as intellectual
strength, perception, problem-solving approaches, physiology, and any
component utilized to gain an understanding of individual behavior.

II. FAMILY THERAPY

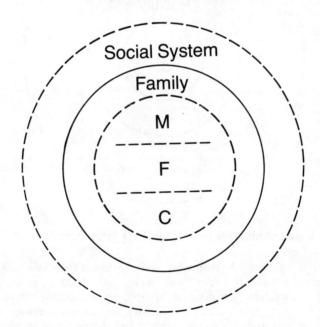

The focus of family therapy is the family as a distinct unit.
Boundaries are hierarchically structured along traditional sex role
lines. Minuchin (1974) writes:

Transactional patterns regulate family members' behavior. They are maintained by two systems of constraint. The first is genetic, involving the universal rules governing family organization. For instance, there must be a power hierarchy, in which parents and children have different levels of authority. There must also be a complementarity of functions, with the husband and wife accepting interdependency and operating as a team. The second system of constraint is ideosyncratic, involving the mutual expectations of particular family members. (p. 52)

Minuchin further clarifies that "the unquestioned authority that once characterized the patriarchal model of the parental subsystem has faded, to be replaced by a concept of flexible, rational authority." (p. 57.) Howels (1971) writes, "Family psychiatry abandons the individual as the unit and adopts the family instead. . . . The loyalty throughout is to the family; the aim is to produce a harmonious, healthy, adjusted family." (p. 57.) Howells further states that, "the clinician has as his endeavor the production of health." (p. 60.) According to Haley (1963) treatment of the family to bring about change and symptom reduction depends upon the therapist's ability to change the total family system. Rather than focus upon intrapsychic conflicts, the therapeutic work involves the context of the relations inside the family. A cybernetic model provides a theoretical framework. Therapeutic tactics are devised in order to resolve intrapersonal power struggles.

Theoretical conceptions span a broad range, from psycho-analytic theory (Ackerman, 1968; Bowen, 1961; Framo, 1962; Howells, 1971; Wynne, 1958) to communication theory and cybernetics (Barry, Hertel, Raush, & Swain, 1974, Haley, 1963; Jackson, 1957, 1965; Minuchin, 1974; Satir, 1964; Watzlawick, Weakland, & Fisch, 1974). Regardless of the theoretical model, the common focus is the reduction of the psychopathological behavior′ of an individual while simultaneously alleviating dysfunctional aspects of family relationships. While the social system is understood to be influential in the production of family stress, therapeutic strategies do not include socio-political issues as important in treatment. This is most clearly stated by Haley (1976).

A therapist can attempt to deal with the social issue by going to extremes. He may define the problem as really a matter of misperception by the client and he may concern himself with the client's fantasies about his social situation. Such a narrow view no longer seems palatable. The therapist can go to the opposite extreme and define all problems as economic and cultural. But then he must become a revolutionary to solve each problem. Such an approach does not seem practical. . . . (p. 5)

The focus on the family, although a radical shift from individual therapy, imposed its model for change upon the family unit. While this treatment approach found many willing families, it did not satisfy those persons who believed that many of their problems were political in nature. Mander and Rush (1974) spoke to this issue:

Therapy seems to me to be one of the ways we in our age have devised to tackle problems we have in dealing with each other and our environment. Therapy can be synonymous with socialization, that is, adjustment to the current cultural model. This seems to be the focus of the psychoanalytic process. However, in other cultures and other areas in western history therapy had had different aims and processes. Today the Chinese use groups as a consciousness-raising tool in their Revolution. I see woman's consciousness-raising groups in America being used in much the same way. (A problem is that only half the population is engaged in the struggle!) I prefer to view therapy as a consciousness-raising process. That is, our getting together to figure out ways we can improve our relating and make some advances in human interaction. (p. 37)

The growth of the women's movement and consciousness-raising was concerned with this flaw in conventional psychotherapy.

III. CONSCIOUSNESS RAISING AND WOMEN'S LIBERATION

Traditional psychotherapy was rejected by the women's movement as a male dominated, sexist form of therapy. Problems in consciousness-raising were explained from the context of one's history, rather than in terms of intrinsic conflict or family power struggles (Gornick, 1971). "I think," write Mander and Rush (1974),

that our existing forms of therapy (clinic, asylums, individual psychoanalysis, the school system) have arisen in response to the breakdown of tribal communities and cohesive extended families. . . . You're learning how to problem solve for yourself by hiring someone else to tell you how; you're learning how to free yourself from outer authority figures by hiring another authority figure. (p. 38)

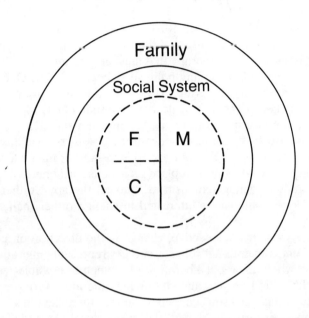

Therapy was seen as an adjustment. Firestone (1970) writes, "The underlying assumption is that one must accept the reality in which one finds oneself." (p. 64.) "As far as the woman is concerned," writes Greer (1970), "psychiatry is an extraordinary confidence trick; the unsuspecting creature seeks aid because she feels unhappy, anxious and confused, and psychology provokes her to seek the cause in herself." (pp. 82-91.) An unsparing criticism is launched upon the theories of psychoanalysis and neo-Freudianism (Firestone, 1970, pp. 41-47; Greer, 1970, pp. 82-92; Hobbs, 1970, pp. 45-58; Mander & Rush, 1974, pp. 37-60; Rowbotham, 1973, pp. 8-9).

The nuclear family is not treated more kindly. Firestone (1970) calls for the abolishment of the nuclear biological family, replacing it with a post-industrial cybernetic socialism where all economic classes and other power hierarchies would disappear. People would seek a livelihood based only on material needs. Greer (1970) sees the family as a primary oppressor of women, writing "Every wife must live with the knowledge that she has nothing else but home and family, while her house is ideally a base which her tired warrior-hunter can withdraw to and express his worst manners, his least amusing conversation, while he licks his wounds and is prepared by laundry and toilet and lunchbox for another sortie." (p. 230.)

According to Mander and Rush (1974), "women and children liberation is the end of culture and the nuclear family as we know it." (p. 50.) It is conventional therapy that must also go under, for "therapy is kept clean and safe from any political stance." (p. 50.) Once again, power is cited as a key issue. However, unlike "power" as it is examined in therapy as a struggle between individuals, power in the context of consciousness-raising is a political issue. That is, write Mander and Rush, "Feminism seeks to bring out the validity of our experience as women so that our experience—rather than what we are told it ought to be—begins to replace erroneous social mythology." (p. 51.) The authors define feminism as "radical therapy" rather than a traditional one; feminism is interested in change rather than "adjustment." (p. 57.)

From the woman's perspective, change in the direction of increased freedom from conventional role stereotypes represents liberation. The problem is whether or not liberation of women is possible without a corollary liberation of men and children. While men were seen as the oppressors, children—still dependent upon their families for nurturance and survival—recreated the hierarchical dependency upon their parents. If a woman could liberate herself from her husband, she found herself in the role of mother, a role in which she was both the oppressed and the oppressor. Even if she chose to leave her family unit, joining with other social units often presented similar political problems to solve. Barber (1975) cites that in America, communes and departmentalized extended families have also presented overbearing, authoritarian leaders. While there are alternative social units that may differ from the nuclear family, "The basic question," writes Hobbs (1970),

is how best to remove or restructure these psychological forces which prevent women from acting as a strong and constructive social force. . . . The question of the "women problem" is not a question of an increase of employment opportunities and legal rights as much as a question of removing psychological blocks. (pp. 76-77)

Finally, writes Barber (1975), "The family is not only a foil in its natural form to the ravages of capitalistic depersonalization, it can also be a bulwark against the encroachment of totalistic states with designs on the autonomy of individual men and women." (p. 64.)

The question is now raised as to whether it is possible to liberate people and still maintain a nuclear family form.

IV. CONSCIOUSNESS-RAISING IN FAMILY THERAPY

By definition, family therapy is understood to be a clinical service. Howells (1971) writes, "for the practice of psychiatry, the family is the unit in referral, in the systemization of symptomatology, in the procedure of investigation and in the processes of therapy." (p. 57.)

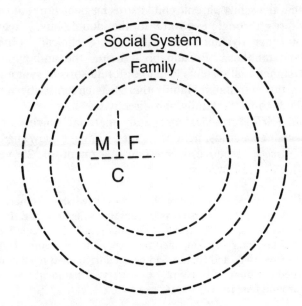

Haley (1963) views symptoms as an intrapersonal way to deal with relationships, a radical departure from traditional psychiatric practice. He also views family therapy as a clinical service as well as a form of treatment. (pp. 151-178.) It is a professional discipline under which a number of mental health practitioners identify themselves, including but not limited to psychiatrists, psychologists, social workers, marriage and family counselors, and other clinically trained psychotherapists.

While a number of family therapists (Auerswald, 1968; Haley, 1963; Minuchin, 1974; Spiegel, 1971) were concerned about the impact that social institutions have had upon the families they treat, the thrust of therapy entailed a clinical analysis and treatment of intrafamilial stress. Symptomatology, particularly when severe, required immediate therapeutic attention. If social conditions have contributed to the etiology of symptomatic behavior, the behavior in and of itself may no longer be a direct response to the larger social context. It is, according to Satir (1971), a response to the system which may be an overruling factor in the use of one's internal dynamics. Further, writes Satir, "it may well be that the system is the primary means by which internal dynamics get developed." (p. 663.) As an example, an analysis of communication processes in families led to the "double-bind" theory, asserting that the schizophrenic child learns his behavioral or communication patterns through exposure to the double-bind situation.[1] A number of other dysfunctional patterns are clinically observed in dysfunctional families. "Presumably," writes the author, "different kinds of dysfunctional systems lead to different sorts of symptoms." (p. 666.) From this standpoint, family therapists circumscribe their treatment methods to fit the family unit directly.[2]

Minuchin (1974) provides case study material which clarifies this issue. Discussing an adjustment of an aged woman to new surroundings (she was forced to move when her apartment of 25 years was ransacked), Minuchin writes:

The frightening experience of unfamiliarity with new circumstances had been interpreted by this lonely person as a conspiracy against her. In the very measure by which she had tried to communicate her experiences, her environmental feedback had amplified her experience of being abnormal and psychotic. Her relatives and friends had become frightened for her and had in turn frightened her by their conspiracy of secrecy. A paranoid community had developed around her. (p. 12)

Describing the treatment intervention, Minuchin writes:

Structural family therapy deals with the process of feedback between circumstances and the person involved . . . the changes imposed by a person on his circumstances and the way in which feedback to these changes affects his next move. A shift in the position of a person vis-a-vis his circumstances constitutes a shift of his experience. Family therapy uses techniques that alter the immediate context of people in such a way that their positions change. By changing the relationship between a person and the familiar context in which he functions, one changes his subjective experience. (p. 13)

The alleviation of symptoms of an individual and the restructuring of a family into a new pattern of relationships may be considered successful treatment, particularly when improved relationships result. In many instances rigid role conflicts may have become more elastic. As a result, the freedom to do different things, to accept or reject long-term responsibilities in favor of new ones, may become a possibility. An overprotective mother described by Minuchin may be encouraged to seek employment. Her husband, becoming more understanding in this regard, permits this to occur and eventually finds his wife's employment a benefit, both financially and in her attitude toward the family. A daughter, once a scapegoat for her mother's overprotective-ness is now freer to grow and relate more effectively to other family members and friends. A better, more harmonious balance has been established. While family members have not changed their viewpoints about what they believe they need, they are more able to work toward the satisfaction of their needs. If many of these needs have been shaped by socioeconomic forces, they remain hidden and entwined within the family's interpretation of reality. Economic pressure to acquire a higher standard of living may be oppressive for a family, but it also works to keep a family functioning together. If there is common agreement that material acquisition represents personal and familial success, a family free of psychological symptoms can function as a closely knit cooperative unit in this regard. While they have not become liberated from social imperative, they have become liberated from the intrafamilial conflicts that blocked their way toward a more harmonious social adjustment.

What, on the other hand, would happen if concurrent with the relief of pathological symptoms family members were encouraged to explore and question many of the socially predetermined imperatives that were driving and shaping their lives? What would happen, for example, if parents long committed to the idea that good parenting requires tight supervision of their children shifted their viewpoint in an opposite direction; that they now considered, as Firestone (1970) remarked, "the best way to raise children is to lay off"? (p. 91.) What would happen to a family if they were not only oriented towards becoming more open, responsible, and affectionate toward one another but collectively questioned and challenged many of the socio-political myths that have determined proper family functioning? Sex roles can be explored, not only with the intent of increasing the flexibility of their definition, but also with the aim of examining whether or not they are naturally interchangeable. Hobbs (1970) explores this issue.

In the current ethos the female pursues and loves the successful man; there is no place in this ethos for the guy who hasn't got it to be loved. According to this ethos it is money, success and title that engender love; for a woman to love a man who does not have these attributes, no matter what his real value as a man, is to fly in the face of the mythology that is currently holding the world of business together. . . . Sex as duty, man as oppressor, spontaneity as un-ladylike—all these images recede before the reality of a total and mutual acceptance of the other. (pp. 120-121)

According to Hobbs:

Modern marriage is a treasury of myth and superstition. . . . The ambitious couple must burden themselves with a home, for instance: whether they need it, want it or can afford it is beside the point. Owning one's home is necessary for the image of permanency and stability which society demands. . . . When there is a house, there next must be children, for in the mythology of business a man's ability to impregnate his wife is closely associated with his virility and creativity. . . . Likewise the success of marriage and parenthood for both man and wife will depend, in the eyes of society, on whether or not the children surpass their parents. . . . The rat race is not only for adults; the little rats must run faster too. (pp. 132-135)

Finally, "the myth is that marriage and parenthood exist for the sake of the children—the fact is that children usually exist for the sake of the parents." (p. 134.)

If family therapy were both to alleviate dysfunctional patterns of communication and to raise questions about heretofore unquestioned assumptions, it would be possible to conserve the family unit while liberating people from deeply ingrained myths. From this perspective, Barber (1975), Hobbs (1970), and Mander and Rush (1974) believe that marriage as a lifelong union between men and women may be possible, though the traditional marriage will be liberated. Hobbs (1970) writes:

Marriage as it is presently idealized is pathological. It is a house of cards built on the foundation of human dreams and overloaded with psychological and material expectations. . . . The institution of marriage in the future can be justified only if it assumes a totally new form and totally new freedoms. (p. 144)

Theoretically, it should be possible to transform the family in such a way that the liberation of individual members and the maintenance of close bonds do not occur at the cost of destroying the foundation of the unit. Barber (1975) believes that this is possible.

He writes:

When it (a family) is healthy, the family can be a vital paradigm of permanent relationships built on uncalculating love and unneurotic commitment. . . . Marriage may in its healthy form be the last institution in the modern era that can still sanction a disinterested mutuality, where it is possible to give without reckoning emotional profit margins, to support without demanding contractual equity, to feel responsible without inquiring about compensation, to love without assuming passion is ephemeral. (p. 67)

It is from this vantage point that the writer presents a series of transcripts of audiotapes of family therapy, wherein treatment of family problems includes consciousness-raising toward the liberation of people in the affairs of family life.

Therapy Transcripts

The transcripts you are about to read have been recorded verbatim from tape recordings made with the family's permission during therapy sessions. Each tape presents that part of the session in which socio-political consciousness-raising has been introduced. Only the first recording encompasses an entire session.

The setting in which these transcripts were recorded was in a state licensed mental health clinic located in the New York metropolitan area. Every family included in this paper has been referred to the clinic from either the public schools or from a recommendation made by a former client. In each case, family therapy was the assigned treatment modality after the family was clinically assessed by an intake worker and, additionally, in some cases by a psychologist who administered a battery of tests to the identified patient. None of the clients was considered to be sufficiently disturbed to warrant a psychiatric examination. Following the initial intake, the writer was assigned the family for therapy. He was introduced to each family as the administrator of family therapy services, as well as a staff therapist. At the first session, each family was informed that recordings would be made with their permission and might be used for a doctoral dissertation on family therapy; if selected, all attempts to respect family anonymity would be taken with the greatest care. Information was not given to the families concerning the theoretical perspective of the work. They were informed that some of the areas the writer would introduce for the dissertation work would have direct bearing upon family concerns as they arose. In response to further questions raised by family members in some cases, the writer informed them that there would be attention paid to forces outside the family, as these forces directly related to intrafamilial problems. In all instances no further information about the intentions of the writer's work was given.

Each transcript will be proceeded by a brief explanation of the therapeutic strategy characterizing the session. An analysis in parallel construction accompanies each transcription. In each analysis the writer has attempted to explain what is going on throughout the session as it was experienced. There was some difficulty in differentiating the therapeutic strategy from the socio-political context in which it was embedded. Responding to this problem, the writer has chosen to work from both ends; that is, the explanations of the session modulate both the treatment strategies and the socio-political issues as they arise.

STRATEGY I: JOINING THE FAMILY SYSTEM

Minuchin (1974) was particularly concerned with a therapist's ability to affiliate with a family in order to change it. He believed that until the therapist was able to become syntonic with the family in treatment, almost any attempt to make an intervention would be met with resistance and guardedness.

Joining the family system is the first and most fundamental strategy necessary in establishing the frame through which change can occur. In this work, the strategy of joining the family was based upon an assessment of the family structure as it characterized patterns of behavior peculiar to a family system's model stage of development.

The shaping of the therapeutic communication style as an operational strategy toward affiliating with a family system takes its form out of the identification with the family's particular stage of development. Joining the family system is a strategy influenced more by stylistic than substantive concerns. Since the operation of joining occurs within the first few sessions of therapy, a primary concern is to establish a sense of kinship and familiarity between therapist and family members.

The Caldwells

This family requested therapy as a result of their 16-year old son's arrest for breaking and entering. This event was the climax of what was described to be a long history of aggressive and incorrigible behavior in the home and in school. As it turned out, Mr. and Mrs. Caldwell were also deeply concerned about their 12-year old daughter who was described as a "liar of the first order." What had occurred in this case was repeated repercussions arising out of the daughter's misinformation regarding events ostensibly unfolding both in school and in her social affairs which later turned out to be unsupported in kind.

The Caldwells were tense and angry as they described their reasons for applying for therapy at the clinic. At the very least, the fact that family court pressured them into seeking therapeutic assistance in the management of their family affairs was an affront to both of them, particularly Mr. Caldwell who, by occupation, was a member of the city police force.

As they recounted the series of transgressions for which their son was responsible, a probe was made toward uncovering the style of their interventions at each disturbing event. It appears that each of their attempted solutions to both children's misbehavior was typically laden with strict unbending punishment, in many instances far out of proportion to the nature of the offense.

The impressions emerging from this interview were:
1. Father was in charge of meting out forceful punishment if and when mother felt herself to be unsuccessful.
2. Father came home from his work generally angry only to be met with a barrage of complaints regarding the children's behavior.
3. Mother was angry at father since he came home tired and angry and was neither in a mood to respond to her bickering nor available to her for support and nourishment.
4. Affection was rarely expressed openly among the members of the family.
5. It was their impression that the school was permissive, uncooperative, and far too lenient with respect to proper punishment.
6. They both felt as though they were failing, but preferred blaming to introspection.

In order to work successfully with this family, the joining strategy demanded that the therapist enter this system by adapting to a rigid "law and order" framework. It was necessary to position oneself inside the family, while remaining outside its boundaries so that control over the interactions remained within the therapist's domain. To accomplish this operation, it was necessary to establish a relationship with the family by recognizing and expressing personal issues similar to those presented by the family.

Changing their belief system began by strategically joining them on an issue followed by a "re-framing" of this issue into a different context. This operation, fundamental to seeding the family for change, remained an ongoing strategy throughout the treatment process. It effectively disarmed the individual of resistance in that it is executed by (a) joining the individual through agreement and consensus and then (b) re-framing the agreement into a counterpoint which challenged the agreement within the same time frame.

The following recorded transcript with the Caldwell family depicts the strategic operation of *Joining and Re-Framing*. The interview is the second meeting and the children are not present. The focus of the interview is to join the family system and begin to re-frame the rigid patriarchical structure governing the family by establishing an affiliation with the father.

The taped portion of the interview follows a brief description Mr. Caldwell is giving of his work on the streets of a ghetto area in the city of New York.

The policemen's occupation and experience are acknowledged as being difficult, as the therapist's position of authority is leveled.

Writer
Being a cop there . . . you really get a slice of life.

Mrs. Caldwell
You can't believe the stories my husband comes home with!

The separation of role requirements (policeman, husband, father) and the difficulty of playing each one is acknowledged.

Writer
I bet it's some tough problem to leave your job when you get home . . .

Mr. Caldwell
I can usually forget it . . . we moved out here to get us and the kids away from the city. It's hard.

Writer
You were a city boy?

Mr. Caldwell
Bronx. It was tough, but now, different.

By establishing common childhood backgrounds, an attempt is made to join the father.

Writer
I came from Brooklyn, Brownsville. I know what you mean. As a kid, I was nervous many a day leaving school. I was a big, strong kid, but that might have been worse. You were a target.

Mr. Caldwell (laughs)
I know what you mean.

Power through affiliation is suggested. Drawing on the father's respect for masculine-type activities, the writer admits he was a football player. The bond between the two is strengthened—first by sex, now by childhood.

Writer
Yeah, I remember if you affiliated with, ah, the really tough guys, or also if you were a member of, say, a school football team, you felt a sense of safety.

Mr. Caldwell (laughs)
You're not kidding.

Writer
I guess this is still true for most kids.

Mr. Caldwell
My son is on the wrestling team, and my wife and I go out and watch him.

Mrs. Caldwell
My husband wouldn't miss it for the world!

The mother's sense of resentment comes through. The husband/son coalition is cemented by physical-combative activities and the mother's comment implies she rates a second to her son in her husband's eyes.

Writer
And you . . . you enjoy going?

Mrs. Caldwell (laughs)
Yes, but not as much as he.

Mr. Caldwell
C'mon, you really get a kick out of seeing him.

Writer
Joe's a powerfully built kid. I noticed that last week. Very muscular. He's probably a good wrestler.

Mr. Caldwell
Could be much better if he worked harder. He's lazy. The coach tells me he's got the power but not the stamina. He doesn't train enough.

Writer
How's he feel about the two of you coming to see him wrestle?

A defense of the son by mother. She identifies with him in a powerless position and by speak-

Mrs. Caldwell
I think it makes him nervous. He never does good enough . . . for

ing of her own unfulfilled attempts to please her husband.

The father's comment is to the writer to strengthen the common male bond—i.e. women cannot understand.

A metaphorical discussion of the father/son relationship is unfolding.

Mr. Caldwell's anger, fear, and helplessness begins to come through.

him. *(Indicates husband.)*

Mr. Caldwell
This is true. And he knows damn well that I can tell when he's in shape. He should'a won the last match, but the other guy wore him down. To me, that's crap!

Mrs. Caldwell
He tried, are you kidding . . .

Mr. Caldwell
If you knew sports, you would know what I mean. Goofing off, he's lazy.

Writer
I know what you mean. I played ball for a coach in high school. An unmerciful guy, drove us through the floor, thought we were a pro team. God, did he ride us.

Mr. Caldwell
That's okay. He knew how to win. And I bet the players respected him.

Writer
Scared of him definitely . . . respect, well, that's another story.

Mr. Caldwell
Kids need fear. If those kids on the street were afraid—learned respect—they damn well wouldn't be dealing dope and screwing at fourteen for pimps.

Writer
Are you saying that if their parents were on the ball, were strict with them, if they really feared their parents, they would not be on the street?

Mrs. Caldwell
That's what he believes.

Writer
You sound unsure?

Sensing an allegiance by the writer's questions, Mrs. Caldwell enters the conversation, diverting the flow in her direction.

Mrs. Caldwell
Well, I grew up with plenty of kids who were afraid of their parents . . . I . . . it's . . . Joey and Carol, they're afraid of us . . . Carol's okay, but . . . Joey's sure not doing too well.

She shifts the issue into the family and adds concern about the father/son relationship.

Writer (nodding agreement)
Mmmmm.

Mrs. Caldwell
Joe is terrified of him . . . !

Mrs. Caldwell makes her point and then turns it into an angry indictment of her husband's relationship with Joey.

Mr. Caldwell
I've belted him when he needed it. But he's not terrified of me. We have a pretty good relationship. Sure he's afraid of me. And he better be. Who the hell will control him? The school sure as hell can't. They keep calling me, complaining. He does this and that, what the hell do you expect? Somebody's gotta let the kid know who is boss.

The manner in which social institutions—school—directly affect family relations is raised. The victimization of both father and son is put forward for exploration. Then, to avoid an indictment of the school system, the writer shifts back to the relations within the family unit.

Writer
You mean that if school was to magically disappear, Joe would be okay?

Mrs. Caldwell
He's gotten in trouble on the street, with his friends. What a crew they are!

Writer
What do you think about that?

Mr. Caldwell
He's a follower. Anything they tell him to do, he'll do. Follows the goddamned crowd, never thinks for himself.

Mrs. Caldwell
That's true.

Rather than permit Joey to be singled out, a shift is made to include the daughter in the discussion. Since the tone of the session is comfortable, it seemed safe to push them further. The shift from school and social concerns goes back into the family. The mother is very concerned with her daughter—and herself—but Joey's overt behavior is allowed to dominate. This permits a focus upon her husband rather than herself.

The focus is shifted from the parent/child relationship to the marriage. The children were not

Writer
If I follow what you've said so far—please correct me if I'm wrong—even though both kids are afraid of you, Joey still gets in a great deal of trouble, and well, Carol, you say she's okay. And in many ways this is true, but you said you're both disturbed about her frequent lying that has caused you embarrassment and concern . . .

Mrs. Caldwell
Mmmmmm.

Writer
Let me switch gears for a mo-

present. To continue the discussion via the children would have allowed the couple to disregard their own relationship and placed the children once again into scapegoat positions. Mrs. Caldwell forms a triangle with the children. The writer detaches her from the triangle.

ment. Do you both see eye-to-eye on your methods of raising the kids?

Mrs. Caldwell
He's too harsh, too strict. He wants everything done his way, by his rules. For me, and the kids . . .
(to husband)
. . . and I've told you that a thousand times.

Writer
How does this affect you?

Mrs. Caldwell
I'm fed up and angry. He comes home very late, angry, exhausted, the whole world stinks and I have to jump. He's got no patience, angry all the time. All the time.

Writer
Have you both discussed . . .

Mrs. Caldwell
I'm sick and tired of telling him the same thing over and over
. . .
(to husband)
. . . but you don't listen. He doesn't listen, and he doesn't change. Every night, bitching about this and . . .

Mr. Caldwell
Do you know what is the . . .

Mrs. Caldwell
Please don't give me that speech again. I have no picnic either. I work too. And I am tired also, but I don't constantly complain. I know his job is rough, lots of things are rough, but you can't always bring them home.

Writer
What effect do you suppose these, ah, issues have on the children?

Mrs. Caldwell
That's easy to see. They're both a mess. And so are we. I'm disgusted with his . . .
(points accusingly)
. . . constant bickering . . . I've told him to quit the force. We can move into . . . there are other ways.

Writer
Have you ever seriously talked about that?

Mrs. Caldwell
A million times . . . he won't budge!

The issue of relocating seemed a remote possibility at this time. Moreover, Mr. Caldwell looked more annoyed with each minute of this discussion. The shift back to present circumstances with attention to change was in answer

Writer
Assuming that you both continue working as you are, and living where you are, what might make a difference for each of you, that would improve some of the ways your family life is right

to that problem. It was readily apparent that their move to the suburbs did not offer magical solutions.

Mrs. Caldwell (laughs)
Are you kidding? If Hal would walk in the door once with a smile once, greet me like a human being . . . ask me how my day was instead of coming home like a wounded tyrant . . .

Mr. Caldwell
C'mon, I don't always . . .

Mrs. Caldwell
You are the angriest man I've ever met! And the kids see it. What can you expect from them? They get what I get. You know what I mean?

Writer
Would you explain.

At this juncture, no connection regarding their circumstances with respect to occupation, economics, etc. is made. Mrs. Caldwell, however, gets closer to expressing her feelings of rejection and loneliness.

Mrs. Caldwell
Sure Hal's affectionate sometimes. He takes Joey out to play ball. We all go out as a family once in a while, but . . . that doesn't make up for what I'm talking about!

Writer
Do you know what your wife means?

Mr. Caldwell (laughs)
I hear it enough!

The difference between hearing and understanding is sharpened.

Writer
Ah, I'm not all that sure that you

At this moment, Mrs. Caldwell and the writer have formed a bond with each other. In order to shift the struggle where caring plays a part, attention to the couple's affection is drawn. The writer speaks to the affectionate and caring side of Mr. Caldwell by pointing out one can be "rough" and yet, gentle. The rough side is then tied to Mr. Caldwell's occupational circumstances. Metaphorically, the discussion centers upon the family, shifting back and forth across the boundaries dividing the social system and the family.

do. Clearly the two of you care a great deal about each other . . . and the children . . . I can see how much you care about them, but I'm not all that sure that you hear each other, and I'm not convinced that you see that what is going on between you is affecting the kids. I want to go back for a moment to our talk earlier about fear and respect. Hal, I can see that you are a pretty rough guy . . . on the other hand, I get the sense that there's a very tender guy struggling to come out—and once in awhile he does . . . Now, as a cop you know how often facing somebody down, making him afraid, only has very short-lived effects. What better example could we have than the prison system? How many guys ruled with fear really change or improve in the prisons? Maybe I'm way off, please correct me if I am, but that, ah, tender guy in you, well, maybe you've learned to hide him, or you've lost him.

Mr. Caldwell
You're damn right.

Writer (to Mrs. Caldwell)
What do you think?

Mrs. Caldwell, touched by what has happened, defends her husband.

Mrs. Caldwell
Of course he's basically a good guy, but look what happens to you, Hal. He was much warmer,

The writer joins Mr. Caldwell by offering a parallel experience. The idea of not being able to express pain through tears is presented as a loss to men. Since Mr. Caldwell already believes that he and the writer are allied, the comment is taken more seriously. Mr. Caldwell makes the connection to his own family of origin as a result of the writer's reference to the closeness of their ages.

The shift to Mr. Caldwell as a child is made in order to help him identify with his son. The implication is that not being permitted to cry, etc., does something unfortunate to men.

Mr. Caldwell's admission was surprising. The writer expected him to, more likely than not, defend his father's parenting as something good and necessary.

much more patient when we met, even when the kids were younger, much more than now.

Writer
It's just incredible what men are taught, what they learn. I couldn't even cry at funerals until I was close to (laughing) thirty years old. That's learned. It's so hard to unlearn. I bet you know what I am talking about.

Mr. Caldwell
My father never allowed us to cry. The boys, that is. He was the meanest son-of-a-bitch this side of heaven.

Mrs. Caldwell (laughs)
He sure was.

Writer
Hal, let me ask you this: what did this do to you, as a kid?

Mr. Caldwell
Well, he always took care of us. You know, food, a home, but I

tell ya, I hated his guts for a long time. My mother, she's a different story. Always protecting us from the old man when he blew his cool. She was a beautiful lady.

Writer
They are not living now?

Mr. Caldwell
No . . . they died when . . . a few years after Carol was born.

The fear issue is reintroduced since Mr. Caldwell has already indicated deep feelings of resentment toward his father. He has not yet connected this to feeling deprived of affection. Only through his mother did he experience affection, in part, his definition of the woman's role.

Writer
I gather you were very much afraid of Papa.

Mr. Caldwell (laughs)
Are you serious? Nobody crossed him . . . and if they did, it only happened once.

Attention is shifted to the identification with his father in order to set up a parallel between his families of origin and of present.

Writer
Do you see yourself as being like him in some ways?

Mrs. Caldwell (smiles)
That's a beauty of a question.

Mr. Caldwell
Sure! Aren't we all like our parents?

Writer
Mmmmm.

Mr. Caldwell
The guy raised me . . . basically with good values . . . a family

man . . . churchgoer. If we missed church he'd break our skull. But he was so goddamned thickheaded. You could never talk to him, never tell him anything that really bothered. You could never show him you were afraid . . . of anything.

Writer
What do you think Papa was afraid of?

Mr. Caldwell had never considered his father capable of experiencing fear.

Mr. Caldwell
If you showed you were afraid . . . or cried, it meant being weak . . . you know, a punk . . . no guts!

Writer
And this was true just for the boys?

Mr. Caldwell
Yeah, women, my mother could be all emotional, you know, cry, or my sister, no problems for them; in fact, my mother was a very emotional woman. She's Italian, my father's Irish Catholic, a perfect match. She used to make a big fuss, but my old man, you couldn't move him . . . though he loved her.

The idea that men are taught to be hard and unemotional is raised for examination.

Writer
So this is what men are supposed to be like!

Mrs. Caldwell (laughs)
Like his father.

Mr. Caldwell
It's hard to answer that.

Writer
Think about it. Don't answer it now. Listen, I think we shared some very important issues here tonight, very important. There's one more question I'd like to ask you, both of you. We spoke about it earlier. Hal, do you . . . and I can be way off here, so please correct me . . . do you see yourself in Joey now?

Mr. Caldwell
You mean is he like me?

Writer
Aha, when you were a kid.

Mr. Caldwell (laughs)
I was one trouble-making son-of-a-bitch!

Writer
Oh . . . ?

Mr. Caldwell (laughs)
Listen, I never said I was a model kid.

Writer (laughs)
So you figure that you'll produce one in your son . . .

Mrs. Caldwell (laughs)
He's some model . . . Mr. Lovable.

Writer

Seriously, a loving, caring papa, that's what you want to be, right?

Mr. Caldwell

No kid . . . no kid's an angel, right?

Writer

I hear you. You mean a kid with good values, one who is responsible, who can be trusted, honest, yes?

Mr. Caldwell

Don't you want the same thing from your kids?

The paradox at this point is that Mr. Caldwell considers himself a man with solid values raised by a man with solid values who was also harsh and punitive. Because father and son are similar types, the notion that punitive parenting does produce "good" children cannot be easily denied. Both Mr. and Mrs. Caldwell are stuck at this point: on the one hand, they've been raised to believe in the aforementioned model; however, the trouble they are having with their children is putting pressure on them to seek an alternative solution. Mr. Caldwell's position as a law officer heightens his frustration and embarrassment. Experiencing this paradox, Mr. Caldwell

Writer

Aha, you bet. Listen, Hal, I can see that, that you people really support these values. Of course, in this, a complex society, it's often a struggle to, ah, live them. Let me ask you this: do you think that fear of punishment, like you described when you were a kid, is this the way to get there, to get a kid to develop these solid values?

Mr. Caldwell

I'm . . . not sure.

Mrs. Caldwell

It's a good question. We sure as hell aren't producing them now!

comes to the rescue of his son, defending the boy's good qualities.

Mr. Caldwell
That's not so . . . you know damn well that they're good kids in a lot a ways . . . You ask Joey to do something and . . .

The writer raises veiled concerns implying that there is more operating than issues about parenting.

Writer
Sure they're good kids. But I think that you and your wife see things here that you're not happy about. I mean, we're here to work out some of the difficulties . . . to look at what may be happening. I think that you've both hit on some very solid things here . . . if it's not a problem leaving them home, I'd like us to meet together again next week, just the three of us. I'd like to get a clearer picture of some of the important issues that we talked about.

Mrs. Caldwell
Fine. We'll be available this time next week.

Their schedule is important and must be taken into account. A fixed weekly appointment cannot be assured since the writer and the family require the flexibility to change time and day when the situation warrants it.

Writer
It's good for me. If it's okay for both of you, I look forward to seeing you then.

(End of interview.)

The following is an excerpted portion of the next interview with the Caldwells. In this session, a more focused effort is made toward examining male-female sex role myths.

An interest and respect for Mr. Caldwell's occupational role is expressed.

Writer
So tell me, Hal, what made you choose to become a cop?

Mr. Caldwell
It's hard to remember. I think it was because a couple of my uncles were on the force, and, ah, it was always something that looked good to me.

Writer
What looked good?

Mr. Caldwell
It was a good, respectable job, you know, decent pay, good benefits.

The idea of a family influence upon the path their children take is raised for exploration.

Writer
Didn't your uncles have an influence on your decision?

Mr. Caldwell
Well, I always looked up to them. Uncle John was my father's brother and my old man always respected John and my great uncle, Pat. They were both given a lot of respect in the family. John did this, Pat did that!

The writer is interested in the wife's influence, prior to their marriage, of her husband's choice of career.

Writer
Did you know them, Vera?

Mrs. Caldwell
Aha. It's like Hal said. They were always very respected in the family. My father-in-law

The writer probes for the delineation of Mr. Caldwell's aspirations, and those of his father. It is important to clarify how much Mr. Caldwell invested toward pleasing his father—a rigid and unaffectionate man—and how deeply this man influenced him.

didn't speak that good about too many people. John and Pat, yes.

Writer
I bet your father was proud as hell when you joined the force, Hal.

Mr. Caldwell
It was like I became the President. My mother was always worried something might happen to me, but my old man was beaming.

Writer
It wasn't easy to get him to beam!

Mr. Caldwell (laughs)
You ain't kiddin'!

Writer
So what did becoming a cop mean to you?

(There is pride in his voice when he states the job is "no picnic.")

Mr. Caldwell
Like I said, it's a job with good pay and good benefits. 'Course, you work for every damn penny . . . it's no picnic!

His anger toward the diminishing status of a policeman comes through rather sharply. The writer is interested in Mr. Caldwell's diminishing sense of power, and how this is translated back into the family.

Writer
The thing that pops into my mind, if I were a policeman, is the power that comes with it.

Mr. Caldwell
Power . . . maybe some years ago, not now, fella. They don't

give a shit if you've got a badge
or not. They'll still tell you to go
fuck yourself, right to your face!

Mrs. Caldwell
My husband's right.

Writer
This wasn't true when you
started on the force.

The loss of power and respect,
once instrinsic to the role of the
policeman, was felt acutely by
Mrs. Caldwell. This was a clue
that in some manner, her stature
as a police officer's wife had also
diminished. The writer's concern
was that she was undercutting
his self-respect as a policeman
while creating greater anger and
resentment in her husband as a
result.

His anger over loss of power and
authority comes through. He felt
his self-respect ebbing, as his
resentment to those in authority
increased. The politicians enjoy
respect and earn a greater salary, all the time the policeman
struggles on the "firing line,"
against a steadily mounting pressure.

Mr. Caldwell
They know goddamn well that a
cop's got to worry about using
his gun now with all the goddamn legislation and politics.
Those sons-of-bitches figure they
got you over a barrel. They can
wise-off and you can't do a
fuckin' thing. The Mayor and all
the bullshit politicians with their
gun control laws and other crap.
Did they ever work the street?
No, they sit on their asses in an
office telling you what to do. If
you get killed, you get a medal
and your family gets a pension.
How's that for bullshit?!

Writer
What do you think about all the
women on the force now?

The writer chose the men/
women issue as one in which
much recent polemic has sur-
faced. The thought was that

women on the force might represent the final undercutting of male power. The writer was concerned not only for this, but over the changes in their marriage as a result.

The issue of women on the beat was a natural point to engage Mrs. Caldwell in the dialogue.

She quickly qualified the remark intimating sexual overtones, to one in which women were a safety hazard to men and were less able to handle themselves in dangerous situations.

Mr. Caldwell
Some are okay. But I'll be goddamned if I'll team up with a woman on my beat.

Writer
What do you think about that, Vera?

Mrs. Caldwell
I don't want a woman with him either.
(laughs)
It's not what you think . . .
(laughs)
It's that a woman can't handle herself in some of the situations Hal gets into. For certain jobs, fine, but not teaming up on the street with what goes on there, not on your life!

Writer
If a woman is a trained police officer, and, ah, is skilled in using a gun and in defense techniques, what difference would it make if you were teamed up with a female?

Mr. Caldwell
Well, even if she was an okay cop, women are too emotional. I know you don't agree with me but they are. That stuff don't go when you're making an arrest. I walk into situations I don't think

a woman should handle. I don't want to go into them, but there are certain things that men should deal with and certain things that women deal with a helluva lot better than men!

Writer
Can you clear this up for me? I'm not sure what you mean.

Mr. Caldwell
There are situations that I want another guy to back me up and he feels the same way.

Writer
I wonder what it would be like if you were assigned a woman partner to patrol with you and she was very good looking, really appealed to you . . .

Mr. Caldwell (laughs)

Writer (continuing)
And here you are, eight hours a day in a car together, eating lunch together, discussing cases together.

Mrs. Caldwell (laughs)
Not on your life!

Writer
I don't know. I think that I'd, ah, really have trouble sorting out my feelings, ah, here I have a professional trained partner,

The writer shifts the issue into the sexual politic and away from the conventional rationalizations about women being less capable than men. This line of reasoning is carried further by suggesting that it is the man who might well have difficulty dealing with his feelings if he were with a woman for a prolonged period of time. Using a personal example, the writer attempts to encourage Mr. Caldwell to feel safe in exploring this issue. It is one rarely expressed openly in marriage built upon conventional sex roles.

and ah, I'm getting all these sexual feelings.

Mr. Caldwell's laughter suggests he is with the writer and is pleased by the writer's personal disclosure.

Mr. Caldwell (laughs)

Writer (continuing)
I can imagine . . .
(laughs)
. . . trying to concentrate on my work and feeling all aroused by this gorgeous gal!

Mr. Caldwell (laughing)
You see why we don't put the guys with the girls on teams!

The opportunity of making a shift to a woman's experience is followed by testing Mrs. Caldwell's willingness to deal with the same issue.

Writer
Vera, what do you think about a situation like that? Here you have a highly skilled police officer—a woman—dedicated to her job, and she's riding with a guy, her teammate, and all the guy can think of is getting her in bed. Isn't that fantastic? Tell me, do you think the same is true of the woman? You know, would she be thinking the same things?

Mrs. Caldwell
A man would have this on his mind much more, definitely, much more . . .

Her response is guarded, and the writer senses her concern by openly discussing this issue from a woman's perspective. This is

Writer
You know it's really funny. What pops into my head is that this team comes on a robbery,

not something she generally does in the presence of her husband and another male. Rather than push her to continue, the writer chooses to construct a hypothetical situation so unjust to the woman, Mrs. Caldwell might be moved to defend her sex.

where they've got to act quickly, and ah, here's the guy daydreaming about making it with his partner. She's ready to move in and he's in this beautiful fantasy. And they escape. It seems to me . . .

Mr. Caldwell (laughs)

Writer (continuing)
. . . that she's the more competent police officer. Yet I bet it gets back that her presence was ah, the detrimental factor, and ah, the failure to apprehend the criminal is seen as a problem in having women on the beat. What do you think?

Mrs. Caldwell joins in, predictably attacking the man for his failing. She does not risk a disclosure that a woman may also be sexually aggressive.

Mrs. Caldwell (laughing)
Ya see, here us women get blamed, and it's you guys all the time. If you'd keep your mind where it belonged . . .
(laughing)
. . . maybe that wouldn't have happened. I never thought of it that way!

Writer
What's worse—you correct me if I'm wrong—the story is told that this chick had the hots for him, distracted him from his work, right? She gets the blame for what has happened either way. Did you ever hear those guys talk in the locker room? You'd be amazed!

Mr. Caldwell (laughs heartily)

Writer (continuing)
Am I right, Hal?

Mr. Caldwell
You're right on!

The writer follows this reasoning and pushes it further into the area of a woman's competency. Although Mrs. Caldwell admits to the possibility that a woman may be a competent police officer, she shifts back to other emotional issues that have challenged the basic beliefs of conventional family life. The pressure experienced by her in light of the changing roles of women threatens her, as it does her husband. She reaches for the issues which have challenged both religious beliefs and those undermining the role of wife and mother. While she defends both, she invests herself in maintaining the family system as it has endured. The dissatisfaction with the marriage, and more, the problems with their daughter, are directly related to the rigid roles and uncompromising rules governing the family system.

Writer
Look at the situation. Here a woman's competency is questioned, right? Because she's a woman. And yet, there are issues about sexuality, that, ah, may have nothing to do with her competency, as a police officer. These issues get stuffed under the rug and people believe that women should not work men's jobs because they aren't as competent. The hidden agenda remains out of consideration, even out of awareness.

Mrs. Caldwell
That's a good point, but you know, these feminist groups go way overboard. Some of the things they say make some sense, but when they start with, ah, things like abortion, and ah, that women who stay home raising kids are good for nothing, this I can't buy. And I resent it . . . it really makes me angry!

(End of taped section.)

Mrs. Caldwell's introduction to the feminist movement seemed an excellent springboard from which to strategically put broad issues into the family system where they could receive personal consideration. The power division in this family was inextricably bound into a rigid internalization of male-female myths influencing both the marital relationships and the relations between parents and children.

Within a short time, two critically important factors emerged and identified the areas of difficulty both children were experiencing.

First, it seemed that Joey was basically an affectionate and tender young man who desperately craved an intimate and warm relationship with his father. His choice of participating in wrestling was to win Mr. Caldwell's approval by acting out what he felt was the only way he could accomplish this desire. As it turned out, his heart was never in wrestling but in less aggressive activities that eventually served a parallel interest for his dad.

Second, the daughter's alleged "lying" was a strategy she designed in order to disguise her sexual feelings and expressions within the peer group. Although she had many questions and concerns, she felt unable to express them to her mother who continued to intermingle harsh antisexual attitudes with a denial that her daughter was developing into a woman.

Therapeutic work proceeded in a direction which explored the effects of the parents' attitudes upon their marriage. Neither was honest with the other regarding their needs and feelings, particularly with respect to their unfulfilling sexual relationship. While Mrs. Caldwell experienced herself as a sexual object, she was unable to accept her own sexual strivings and in effect, did not enjoy the sensuality of her own body or a feeling of intimacy with her husband. Mr. Caldwell separated "women" from the dual role of wife/mother or women as sexual objects and, in effect was dutifully and mechanically sexual with his wife. This resulted in a deeply unfulfilling relationship and feelings of anger and isolation from Mrs. Caldwell.

At this writing, therapy with the Caldwells continues to examine the internalized socio-political myths that shape the developing family system.

STRATEGY II: Economics and Autonomy

In addressing issues that particularly support rigid patriarchy in a family system, the economic arena is fundamental and assumes pointed emphasis in socio-political consciousness-raising. The control and dispersion of money predetermines the control and dispersion of power within the family system. This is particularly true if and when the father is the only paid supporter of the family members.

The understructure of this situation is based upon long-standing socio-cultural myths responsible for romanticizing the sanctity of the maternal role but, in actuality, subjugating both women and children to positions of dependency and powerlessness.

An outcome of this understructure is the nexus established between economic dependence and sexuality. In working with many families where economic issues assumed forefront emphasis, it was not difficult to envisage just how clearly these issues pointed to sexual tensions and dissatisfactions. In no uncertain terms, many family squabbles had their roots in the hidden reality that the mother perceived her role as a "kept woman." This was true both in the areas of dutifully responding to her husband's sexual needs as well as the inability to survive on her own if and when the marriage was to go sour. Oftentimes, the mother's employment, particularly if, when it was rewarded handsomely in salary, threatened her husband's security vis-à-vis his power and control over the maintenance of their relationship. After all, if the woman could prove her self-sufficiency, then they would remain as a married couple more out of choice than obligation.

From this point of view of the parental relationship with the children, similar issues of subjugation exist. In many families keeping the children dependent upon parental authority is a major goal in order to control or monitor the children's lives. Therein, children obtaining their own financial sources smack of an independence which many parents cannot willfully tolerate. As a result, they demand that their children relinquish the jobs they might have and concentrate upon the "more important" responsibilities such as school. To augment the children's income, the parents regulate an allowance which in many cases is based on a number of contingencies. If the children transgress in their responsibilities, the allowance is automatically adjusted accordingly.

The Sterns

The Sterns entered family therapy upon the advice of a school psychologist who had recently interviewed their 12-year old daughter. She presented a long-standing picture of academic failure despite a measurably high intellectual evaluation. There were no observable features that would account for Debra's poor school performance, as evidenced by the testing. The parents were perplexed since they had previously invested large sums of money for tutorial help for Debra, though results continuously proved fruitless.

Frustration and anger finally overcame their resistance toward psychological counseling and, after much prodding, they accepted family therapy on a trial basis.

Mr. Stern is a successful accountant. His wife, Edna, had recently gone back to work in a clerical position both arguing that her working did not signify that her husband was less than a competent provider for her needs.

Their relationship with Debra was to a noticeable extent distant and rigidly demanding. The demanding quality pervaded almost every observable area of family life. While decrying Debra's failures and irresponsibility in performing her duties as they defined them, they offered this youngster no avenue for autonomy and independence. Control was absolute and Debra simply danced as they choreographed her routines. Only in her school work were they unable to assert their combined authority and achieve the results they craved. Debra had clearly seen to that.

The following conversation occurred at the fourth family session. In attendance were Mr. and Mrs. Stern and Debra. The springboard to this conversation was Mr. Stern's obvious dissatisfaction with his wife's new-found employment. The transcript presented has been excerpted from the full interview.

After placing his wife in the position of a "nag," Mr. Stern sends out a double message: what he says and what he means are at odds. Mrs. Stern responds to this by acting on what he says and the argument progresses. Their daughter, Debra, is systematically introduced into the conflict by both parties to raise whatever guilt is necessary in order to win a point. Thus, when either of them acts on his intentions, the act is always intertwined in guilt that is sys-

Mrs. Stern
You have not stopped complaining about my working for one minute. You told me fine, get a job if that's what I wanted. I get it and you continuously harp on me. I am sick.

Mr. Stern
She's blowing the whole thing way out of proportion. I have said, complained, about not working, but since she began, Debra's work, schoolwork has taken a nosedive, and . . .

tematically used by the other party.

Mrs. Stern's frustrations with her oppressed role is typified by Debra's failure to respond. In the three sessions already conducted, this couple rarely confronted one another without introducing their parental role or some other indirect issue.

Mrs. Stern attacks her husband for disapproving of Debra's friends—but this is really her position. Mr. Stern uses that argument as a means to control his wife: he appears to support her, but can turn around and say, "Haven't I been a good parent?"; etc.

The issue of Debra's friends is one in a string of ways they control their daughter's autonomy and independence. During all of this, Debra sits, appearing distant and looking like a hopeless captive.

The writer attempts to bring Debra into the dialogue by exaggerating the point of her parents' argument.

The writer, concerned lest Debra believe the comment, shifts

Mrs. Stern
Sure. Debra's work is poor because I'm working.
(angry, sarcastic tone)
You would like me to sit with her like a policeman, right? I should sit with her and force her to do, to study, and you, you come home to the castle, have a drink, expect dinner, right, and I am, I'm supposed to be a machine. A lot of good me sitting with her has done. I used to get daily reports from the teachers. I sat on her like a pancake. It worked, right?
(sarcastic tone, looking at husband)
Maybe we should stop her from seeing her friends. You can't stand half of them anyway. Okay? Should we do that, big shot?

Debra (sits listening, expressionless)

Writer (turning to Debra) So, what do you think about this, Deb? Maybe a good spanking would work . . . (smiling)

Debra
I don't think . . .

Writer
I'm not really seriously suggest-

to its humorous intent and, sensing the mother's frustrations, calls attention to that. The idea that Mrs. Stern does not think of Debra as an incapable child is suggested.

The focus is shifted to the mother. This triangulates the family problems and removes Debra from the scapegoat position. It is hoped that Debra will now feel safe and participate.

The shift is pushed even further, indicating: (a) it is, in part, the mother's struggle, and (b) the daughter is implicated in this struggle.

Mrs. Stern perceives this and suggests that her daughter would profit by increased freedom.

By inviting the father to join the dialogue, the triangle is again alluded to by the writer.

This line of thinking is encouraged by giving the mother credit for introducing it. Mrs. Stern, feeling the support, continues and implicates both herself and her husband. Guilt, a favorite

ing a spanking, and neither is mother . . .

Mrs. Stern (chuckles)

Writer (continuing)
Listen, this one could put you on the spot. So you can take, ah, the Fifth Amendment. But I'll ask you. What's your feeling, ah, about mother working?

Debra (expressionless)
It's okay.

Writer (laughs)
See, here you have permission from Deb to continue.

Mrs. Stern (laughs)
Sure, you blame her? She's a lot better off with both of us off her back out of the house.

Writer
What do you think, Dad?

Mr. Stern (shrugs in a noncommital gesture)

Writer (continuing)
Listen, you might have a point there, Edna.

Mrs. Stern (laughs)
How would *you* like us as par-

means through which issues are explored, is reintroduced. Mr. Stern immediately responds in kind.

Mrs. Stern continues in this vein by citing their failures as the reason people engage in therapy. There is little doubt that successful parenting means a happy child who does well in school.

The writer, not yet joined in a relationship with Debra, uses humor to draw her closer. This also triangulates the problem.

The shift returns to the issue of Mrs. Stern's recent employment. Independence is the key issue, and it is thought that Debra will participate if she is not maintained as the symbol for Mrs. Stern's struggle with her husband. The use of first names is preferred for increasing intimacy, and leveling power.

The writer decided to point out the rule disallowing interruptions.

ents?

Mr. Stern
Jesus, you make it like we're the worst people . . .

Mrs. Stern
So, we're here in therapy. Why? Because we did a good job?

Writer
This is a good question, perhaps . . .

Mrs. Stern
Because she's a wreck. And she fails and we sit on top of her, and, ah, look at her. Did you ever see such a miserably unhappy kid?

Writer (laughs)
So, Deb. Is there anyone as miserable and unhappy?

Debra (chuckles at the comment)

Writer
Edna, does Elias know why you are really working?

Mr. Stern
I can . . .

Writer
Wait a moment. Sometimes we have so much to say. Please

The issue of Mrs. Stern's struggle for independence and autonomy surfaces sharply. Although it is not the first time this confrontation has occurred between the couple, it is the first time in therapy.

Mrs. Stern gives the writer the title of "Doctor." She felt some support, and increased the power of her ally.

The writer moved to involve Debra because she is the mother's substitute. This substitution is heightened by requesting Debra to clarify the issue. It was also an experiment to see how Mr. Stern would react; since he really does not listen to his wife, one wonders if he might listen to his daughter.

listen, then you can comment. Okay? Even if you disagree while someone else is talking.

Mrs. Stern
I'm working to get out of the house. I'm sick and tired of being a maid, and I'm sick and tired of asking you . . .
(faces husband)
. . . for a few dollars each and every time I need something. And please don't tell me you give me enough money. A hundred times you said that and a hundred times I told you that's not the reason.

Mr. Stern
So what . . .

Mrs. Stern
Would you believe him, Doctor?
(fed up gesture with hand)
Would you believe this man still doesn't understand?

Writer
Deb, can you explain to your father what your mother means?

Debra (appearing surprised)
She wants to have a life of her own.

Writer
Wow, that is one right-on comment on your mother's position. Could you go on?

It is a rare opportunity for Debra to participate in a serious conversation that does not center on her schooling.

Debra
Daddy gives her enough money to, ah, you know, take care of the house and all, but . . .

Writer
But . . .

Debra
My mother wants to, er, have, ah, she wants to be independent, you know, so she doesn't have to keep asking Daddy when she wants a pair of shoes, or a dress.

Mrs. Stern (nods approvingly)

The writer, sensing Debra's anxiety about crossing over the boundaries permitted her, gently encourages her to continue.

Writer
Deb, are you trying to tell me that women, ah, women need to feel independent like men, and ah . . .

Debra (nods with gesturing agreement)

Writer (continuing)
And your mother is working so that she can feel freer in her own life . . .

The allegiance between Mrs. Stern and her daughter tightens. Although Debra is speaking to the writer, Mr. Stern is paying very close attention. Debra does glance at her father, but eye-contact is not sustained.

Debra
She's tired of just staying home and cleaning . . .

The idea of freedom by choosing work, a situation where other demands are made, is questioned in order to explore the experience of independence from different angles.

Writer
You think getting up every morning and, ah, having to report to an office where you have a boss to answer to is giving her more freedom? Does that sound free?

Debra
It's better than . . . staying home and . . . ah . . .

Mrs. Stern
And having to beg for . . .

Mr. Stern
Beg?! You've got to be kidding!

Mrs. Stern
All right. I don't beg. I admit you give me enough money to, er, take care of . . . I can't complain.

The writer anticipates that the money issue can lead to a heated argument familiar to the family. Since the issue concerns freedom, independence, and autonomy in a battle of sex-role definitions, the writer suggests hidden issues and raises the thought that this is what Debra was speaking about.

Writer
I never thought otherwise. I think Deb was pointing out some other issues.

Mrs. Stern
It's impossible for men to understand. There's a sense of independence about working even if you have to follow . . . ah, even if you have to comply with the . . .

Mrs. Stern is quick to seize upon this since her employment has afforded her new found freedom.

The writer, sensing that Mrs. Stern is stuck, chooses to sharpen the issue by reversing sex-role experiences. To draw Mr. Stern into this, it was important to acknowledge his professional status. The choice to focus upon nonmonetary gains which come from skilled and competent work further diminished the issue of money—which is not at the heart of this argument.

Using this point also introduced the idea that money, although important, is not the sole reason people choose to remain in an occupational role. If money is separated from this, it can later be addressed as a means through which independence is gained, even if work is not fulfilling in and of itself.

The similarity of Mr. Stern's and the writer's childhood is introduced in order to (a) increase an

Writer
Elias, can you imagine just for a moment what it would be like if, ah, you switched positions? I mean, I can see that you are a serious and successful professional. And ah, along with monetary rewards that, in a way, at least in this culture, suggests that you are good at what you do. I sense that there's a personal satisfaction you get—I may be wrong, so please correct me— from the competent work you do, a feeling maybe of personal achievement?

Mr. Stern
That is certainly true.

Writer
What do you think? Do you think Edna may have a similar need as a woman?

Mr. Stern
I guess so, uh, you know, you get used to . . . a certain way of living.

Writer (laughs)
Don't I know. I think our childhood was, ah, quite similar in these kinds of issues.

Mr. Stern (nods in agreement)

Writer (continuing)
. . . that, ah, times certainly have changed.

allegiance, and (b) point out that what was once true for both may no longer be true now. It joins both men in the struggle.

The writer takes the position of reframing Mr. Stern's resistance as something positive between the couple, implying that Mrs. Stern, too, has had a part in this dependency bond.

The writer pays a compliment to Mrs. Stern, indicating that he can understand why her husband chooses to be possessive. The shift is then made in order to explore the threat a woman's independence could mean to a man. Mr. Stern surprises the writer by acknowledging this fear.

The idea that Debra's good grades are in her control, and represent a reward to her parents is introduced. This sets the stage for exploring the issue of autonomy and the resentment that surfaces when freedom is limited and controlled by someone else. It is implied that Mrs. Stern and Debra have a common struggle.

Mr. Stern
You're not kidding!

Writer
Edna, I may be wrong, but it seems that some of Elias' resentment over your working is, ah, because he . . . he really wants you around, you know, he misses your company and being taken care of . . .

Mrs. Stern (laughs and nods)
He's such a baby.

Writer
Well, you know he doesn't have to be a baby to want to be with you. Elias, have you told Edna that you don't want to share her . . . with anyone else?

Mr. Stern (laughs)
This is true.

Writer
I must say, I was right from the start to be impressed with how much the two of you really care about each other. And, ah, I can see how much you both, ah, care about your daughter. But as things stand now, Deb is just not going to give you the pleasure of good grades. No, she is just not ready to do that yet.

Debra (listens intently)

Mrs. Stern
I never thought of it that way.

Writer
No, she's just not ready to do that. Mmm, you can turn her upside down and give her tutoring on her head, that hasn't done it, right?

Mr. and Mrs. Stern (both nod)

The writer lays the groundwork for later explorations of children's rights and parents' responsibilities. The issue of control by refusal is a good one to center on—it also depicts the couple's struggle for intimacy and freedom.

Writer (continuing)
You see, no matter what you do, in the way that, ah, you have looked at school, this is, ah, something, an area where Deb has complete control over herself. I mean, you can't jam learning down anyone's throat, right?

Mr. and Mrs. Stern (affirmative nods)

The writer alludes to the child's power as an oppressor when told to grow within diminishing freedom. There is reference to the "games people play" in order to fool authority figures.

Writer (continuing)
You can lock her up in her room, make her look like she's studying . . . sit with her, hire the world's best tutor . . . it won't do a damn bit of good unless Deb is ready, on her own, to do well at school.

Debra (nods, listens intently)

Writer (continuing)
Now, this may sound strange.

The writer underscores Debra's right to fail and counters the thought that there may be other ways to achieve freedom.

In this regard, the idea of doing well in school is not discouraged, and the parents can then safely explore the idea presented without feeling overly threatened. Mrs. Stern's comment indicates how much their responsibility as parents is tied into the school.

While Mr. Stern does not grasp the theme of children's rights, he does allude to the struggle in the context of his relationship with his wife.

Please, if you disagree, let me know and we'll discuss it. What I want to tell you is, and you may thoroughly disagree . . .
(pause)
. . . Debra has an absolute right to fail!
(pause for emphasis)
Don't misunderstand me now, I am not advocating doing poorly. I am not suggesting that this is a good road to take in order to solve our problems. Nope, I am simply saying that she . . .
(pointing)
. . . has a right to fail!

Mrs. Stern
I guess that's ah, true, but, I never looked at it that way. Ah, where does this leave us?

Writer (laughs)
It leaves us right where we are. Elias, what do you think about what I've said?

Mr. Stern
I've told, ah, Edna, forget it already. If she fails, she fails. What's the sense of, ah, driving ourselves crazy over her grades. They don't get better, we just fight over them.

Writer
Well, I agree with you there. But, ah, I'm making another statement. What I'm saying is that she has a choice, a right to fail. How does that strike you?

Mr. Stern
This, I . . . it could be true.
(laughs)
But my parents would never agree with you in a million years. Also, what about, ah, our responsibility as, ah, her parents? . . . Should we just turn our backs and let her fail? Suppose she doesn't even finish high school, is this proper for her parents to do—to let her go to the dogs?

The strength of inter-generational influence is clear as Mr. Stern cites his own parent' disapproval of him, were he to decrease his parental duties in child-raising. The writer acknowledges the difficulty in clarifying this issue, but decides to focus on it since all family members seem most interested and involved. Where adolescent females are concerned, sexual issues are often central ones, and the writer shifts to this area. It appears that Mrs. Stern's comment about kids running "hogwild" influenced the writer at that moment to make the shift.

Writer
I think that you're raising a critically important question: ah, what in fact are the responsibilities of parents, any parents, toward their children? And, also, what are the responsibilities that, ah, children have toward their parents and, of course, their own lives?

Mrs. Stern
Well, you have to guide them, and, ah, point out important things that will set them on the right path for, ah, their future, right?

Writer (nods, as a listening cue without comment)

Mrs. Stern
You can't let kids run hogwild.

The sexual issue was introduced primarily as a concern between the parents. The comment im-

Writer
Have the two of you spoken about the sexual concerns and

plied that sexual concerns were not only focused around their daughter, but involved in their marriage as well.

As expected, freedom is automatically equated with sex, since sexuality is a loaded issue. It usually is a primary concern, particularly when birth control methods are so available to young people. The subject is also the least openly spoken about topic in many middle class homes between parents and children, save erotic jokes, a passing reference, etc.

Mrs. Stern quickly makes an association to herself suggesting they have, in some manner, struggled over her increasing freedom.

fears that, ah, are obviously worrying you?

Mrs. Stern (eyes widening as she pauses contemplatively)
Well, er . . . not, ah . . . right out . . . but, ah, yes, I am worried . . . ah, you know what goes on with kids . . . who—are free and, er, are not, ah, made to toe the mark, you know, who stay out all hours and hang around on the corner. Sure I'm worried, and believe me, with good cause.

Writer
Elias, it doesn't matter what age a woman is, if they have freedom men are worried about what could come of it.

Mr. Stern (looks surprised)

Mrs. Stern (smiles, as if she has made the connection between herself and her daughter)
Oh, aha, I get you . . .
(very pleased)
I get you. Elias, he's telling you that you are worried about me like we are worried about Deb!
(laughs)

Writer (laughs)
SO!

Mr. Stern (laughs, but says nothing)

The writer ends the session knowing the freedom-equals-sex issue will be a central one the following week. The comment to both women was gently introduced in order to sharpen the idea that men will undoubtedly be drawn to Mrs. Stern as well as her daughter.

Writer
You're both very attractive women.

Mrs. Stern (laughs)
You devil!

Writer
We must break now. Is this a good time for you or would you prefer an hour later?

(Everyone rises and heads slowly to the door. An appointment time is agreed upon and the session abruptly ends.)

This interview brought the Stern family to the edge of examining issues which essentially have shaped the family cosmology. Their combined efforts to write the script for Debra's life was a fabric woven into a complex set of rules and regulations governing the interactional patterns of their relationships.

Control over Debra was strangling all of them in different ways. Deb is a bright, alert, and relatively sophisticated young lady. She is not only aware of the waves of social change but has slowly begun to explore and assimilate them into herself. She was touched by her mother's growing awareness of the value of independence counterpointed with her father's resistance and trepidation for what that independence might represent.

Essentially, Mr. Stern was struggling to maintain the family forms with which he was secure; therein, he turned in desperation toward his wife in an attempt to enlarge her guilt over her new-found employment by emphasizing that this was resulting in Debra's downfall. Frightened, he used Debra who had been a convenient lever to control Mrs. Stern. Since her school failure had been long term, and since Mr. Stern harbored the rigid male-role belief that the mother is responsible for raising the children, particularly so in the case of a daughter, he was in a fairly solid position to work on his wife's guilt.

Mrs. Stern, frightened over her growing need for autonomy counterpointed with her internalized conventional family morality, turned toward Debra as a lever to work out her own problems. If Debra would simply please her (after all she has done) and perform well in school,

Mrs. Stern could free herself from the strangling situation in which she was trapped.

For Debra, this meant that she would have to respond in a favorable way toward her mother's increasing pressure upon her. She had never totally yielded to her parents' attempts to control her, particularly with respect to school work. Feeling her mother's pressure and sensing her position as a pawn to free her mother, she entrapped herself more rigidly and would not budge an inch. Debra saw nothing favorable coming out of this for herself.

The therapeutic strategy following this session focused upon the importance of independence, notably financial independence, as a release from pernicious antifemale myths governing family life. For the Sterns, it was important to work out the mother's need for independence through her employment while positioning this action as a factor that could strengthen relational ties within the family. This was also true with Debra, who eventually got a part-time job and at the same time improved her school performance dramatically.

STRATEGY III: PARADOXICAL AND DOUBLE-BIND TACTICS IN SOCIO-POLITICAL CONSCIOUSNESS RAISING

The work of Watzlawick, Weakland and Fisch (1974) and Haley (1963, 1976) presented a fascinating series of examples demonstrating how change is generated by shifting attention to the futility of changing the person and the family system. Assigning outlandish and seemingly unrelated tasks to his patients, Milton Ericksen, as described by Jay Haley in *Uncommon Therapy,* produced a startling and abrupt termination of symptoms. Haley and the others demonstrated the force of a therapeutic double-bind: a therapist giving a suggestion would achieve his intentions whether or not the patient obeyed. Prescriptions and other tactics aimed at altering behavior were frequently delivered in a form which required the patient to exaggerate the very behavior he or she desired to change.

The idea of utilizing these tactics adapted to socio-political consciousness-raising proved to be instrumental in generating changes in behavior. Consideration had to be leveled at distinguishing "change" as it occurs in therapy from "change" as it is defined out of a consciousness-raising experience. The former is primarily concerned with alterations of behavior within the family system regardless of whether or not an awareness of the factors producing change has been achieved. In the latter, change is fundamental to an awareness and follows a raising of consciousness (awareness) to particular forms of behavior and issues.

This distinction influenced the researcher toward using a paradoxical tactic to generate change followed with issues pertaining to internalized socio-political myths later to be examined.

The Simpsons

The following portion of a taped interview demonstrates the use of a paradoxical tactic positioned within the body of a therapeutic session. The father, an attorney, was inflamed and unbending when it came to the definition of male-female role behavior. Present for this session are Mr. and Mrs. Simpson and their 16-year old daughter, Judith.

Mr. Simpson
I make a damn good income. I am sick and tired of arguing about Martha going to work. I didn't break my back going to law school and working 6 days a week for my firm to have my wife go out and get paid $2.00 an hour selling cosmetics in a department store. When she worked I used to come home exhausted and expected dinner and a little, ah, a drink, some intelligent conversation . . . and when Martha walked in, she was exhausted; every night I came home to a corpse. And this is not what I broke my back for. And she knows it's true. Right, tell him. Weren't you dead tired when I walked in the door? No dinner for me, Judy forgot who her mother was.

Mrs. Simpson
Hal, we already went into it.

The issue of the male patriarch as king of his roost is experienced through Mr. Simpson. He has successfully achieved the trappings of the suburban dream, only to discover his women neglecting him and her responsibilities. If indictment of personal neglect by his wife failed, he pointed the finger toward her neglect of their daughter, evoking the bad parent issue, a tactic which often worked to his benefit.

The writer had introduced himself as "Dr." and asked to be referred to by first name. Utilizing the title of "doctor" is often done when a client wants the added weight of authority on his side.

The writer feels close enough to the family to introduce a paradoxical tactic with an edge of satire. Had this comment just described Mr. Simpson's wife, he might have agreed; however, his strong desire and feelings for his daughter, to become an educated and successful woman would not allow Mr. Simpson to sit in agreement. When the writer linked the sex-role behavior to the daughter, Mr. Simpson's facial expression clearly changed. Before he could respond, Judy, the 16-year old, jumped into the dialogue, indignant and shocked that the writer

Mr. Simpson
Doc, am I right? Is it too much to expect? Am I wrong in wanting my wife alive when I come home? Judy, she'll tell you how the whole business was. And we're both tired of it—and my wife's starting again, now a cosmetic salesgirl. Next she'll apply for a job as a housemaid!

Mrs. Simpson
Now, let's not get smart, mister, or maybe I will, at that!

Writer
Hal, you've got some solid points here! As a matter of fact, I'm surprised that a guy like you ever let Martha work in the first place! A woman like Martha belongs in the house. She really has no other saleable skills. Women should stay where they belong, and cater hand-and-foot to their husbands. After all, you went to law school to provide a nice home for her. For God's sake, the least Martha could do is keep it clean all day, and when you get home make you as comfortable as possible, so you can go to work the next day and the next day after that in order to keep your family well cared for. This is certainly a woman's role, and, ah, Judy will learn this as soon as she's married. In fact, I sometimes wonder why the hell girls are sent to school altogether.

could ever confirm such an unspeakable description of a woman's role in life. Since she believed the writer's comment, it seemed worthwhile to continue the maneuver. It was Mr. Simpson who could not accept the description and judged it to be tongue-in-cheek. The writer, guessing Mr. Simpson was uncertain, assumed an attitude of surprise when accused of intentionally putting him on.

Mr. Simpson, still uncertain, takes the serious view and in a moment of self-reflection calls himself a chauvinist. This was an invitation for Mrs. Simpson to enter the dialogue. She, too, was uncertain of the writer's seriousness, yet the comments hit home for her. She chose to challenge her husband, indicating an awareness on her part that the writer was deliberately provoking them.

At this moment, Mr. Simpson chooses to refer to the writer by first name, of his own accord.

Judy
That's unbelievable!

Writer
It's a complete waste . . . men need a woman's care . . . even the few nights Martha goes out with her friends shocks me. (to Mr. Simpson) If she had more appreciation for everything you do for her, ah, it seems to me that she'd stay home and keep you company, and make you comfortable. What other needs could any woman possibly have?

Mr. Simpson (laughs)
You're putting me on . . .

Writer
Huh?

Mr. Simpson (laughs)
I know you don't mean, ah, are you kidding? You make me sound like the worst bastard chauvinist!

Mrs. Simpson
You said it, not me, Hal . . . (laughs)

Mr. Simpson
Are you kidding? You agree with him that, ah, that's what I expect. I don't believe you could say in all honesty that, ah, what

Neil said, that my—that that's
what I expect out of you and
Judy.

Judy
Daddy, that's really what you
sound like.

Writer
Hal, do you mean I didn't hear
you correctly . . . ?

In the Simpson family, the use of this tactic served as a pivotal point
from which an examination of the power-relations between the parents
unfolded. Since these people were relatively sophisticated, the tactic
dramatized the "absurdity" of the husband's stance, while defusing
some of his resistance to willingly examine and understand the effects
his position was having upon his family system. A more direct approach
would have invited him to engage in a counter-argument, something he
was particularly skilled at doing, in order to avoid introspection and
sensitivity.

A second example of a paradoxical double-bind intervention was
utilized toward releasing a father from his lifelong belief that anatomy
is destiny for men.

The Combs

George Combs refused to get close to his 3-year old son. It was his
contention that boys are weakened through indulgence, which he
blindly interpreted to mean affection. Since Mrs. Combs was part of
this parental dyad she reinforced George's belief by double-binding
him. On the one hand, she complained of little help from her husband
in raising their son and, on the other hand, she covertly supported
George's stance. As a result, Mrs. Combs managed to keep her
husband outside the perimeter of the relationship she had with their
son, Patty. Although George felt envious and rejected, he could only
express his feelings obliquely and hostilely. The following brief
conversation illustrates a strategic paradoxical intervention positioned
in order to unhook the parental dyad from their internalized childrearing myths.

The scene in which this interview occurs is all important to the strategy. Seated on two hard-back chairs approximately two feet apart are Mr. and Mrs. Combs. In accord with the previous week's instructions, they brought 3-year old Patty into the family session. The preplan was that the writer would have available a few choice toys, crayons, and large paper which would be used as a play session between the writer and the child.

As the interview progresses, the writer is seated on the floor playing with the 3-year old boy while Mr. and Mrs. Combs look on.

Due to difficulties in transcribing this tape verbatim, the interaction between the writer and the child is omitted. The interaction included a great deal of laughter and touching going on between the pair. The following conversation unfolded during the play session.

Mrs. Combs was the spokesperson for the child—not only for what he wished to say, but for what his actions represented and expressed.

Mrs. Combs
He loves to color. Patty, show the man how you make a tree. Go ahead. Show him, Patty. We always color together. I bought him some coloring books. Show the man, Patty. He's trying to stay in the lines now. That'sa boy.
(smiling)

The smile was tight and it was obvious she had much invested in Patty's performance.

Writer
Look at that. Boy, that is terrific! Terrific. How's that, George. This guy's really talented . . .
(laughing)
. . . George, could you imagine if you had a daughter? Then you could play also. But what can you do? Some things you just can't control!

The writer chose to disentangle the mother/child coalition by addressing his remarks to the father. The remark about the father having a daughter to play with was a provocative one. It challenged Mr. Combs' alienation from his son as well as the idea that playing with a male child would tend to feminize him. As the conversation continued, the writer interacted

Mrs. Combs
Not on the rug, Patty. Patty, color on the paper. That's a good boy!

with the child, who freely expressed his joy and excitement. Introducing the writer's family removed the interplay between the writer and child from the professional arena. This device played down the idea that the interaction was occurring as a result of the writer's professional responsibilities.

Writer
A boy needs a strong male model. I know just how you feel. I have a 6-year old son. I'm forever amazed at how my son Andy copies everything I do. He even uses choice words of mine. It's just incredible how great an influence we have on our kids. That's beautiful, Patty. Boy that is really a beautiful tree!

Patty (beams with pride)

Writer (continuing)
Gloria, you're right. This guy's got some talent, here!

Mrs. Combs (laughs)
I told you. George, isn't that good?

Mr. Combs (sits rigidly observing)
Aha.

(Patty picks up a doll lying next to him and begins exploring it. Mrs. Combs asks him to name the parts of the body.)

A boy with a doll is suggested as a masculine activity for the male part in child-raising. Although Mrs. Combs admits to never considering giving her son a doll, she makes it appear as though, if it were not for her husband, she would approve of it. Clearly she was communicating her value to

Writer
Have you given Patty a doll so he can help you with the new baby?

Mrs. Combs
No, I never thought of it. But George would die if Patty played with a doll, right, George?

Mr. Combs and teasing him at the same time.

Mr. Combs
Would you want him to?

Mrs. Combs (laughs)
Maybe it wouldn't hurt *you* any.

The writer shifts the level of the dialogue in response to a sense of pain in both of them. Once again, a monologue was utilized to cover a number of issues which could synthesize Mr. Combs' experiences. They are: (a) that love and affection from father to son is okay; (b) that deep feelings of love are often frightening; (c) that affection and love sometimes make us vulnerable; (d) that a man is safer if he hides these feelings—but paradoxically, he is not more of a man, he is not stronger.

Writer
Ah, on the contrary, it's often very painful to be close, to express deep feelings of love and affection to your child. I remember holding my son in my arms when he was about two, rocking him alone in my arms in his room and suddenly I felt an overwhelming sadness and love. It was frightening. I became aware for that one moment of my vulnerability. Up until that time, I thought in my magical thoughts that I was Superman's brother . . . you know what I mean . . .

Mr. and Mrs. Combs (both nod)

This session initiated a restructuring of the father's relationship with his son. Following sessions helped the entire unit to play together, and as a result, increased the intimacy between the couple. Mrs. Combs was made aware of her role in maintaining the dyad with her son, thus keeping her husband on the outside as an observer.

Writer (continuing)
. . . that nothing could ever happen to me. Not me. But holding my son I suddenly realized how much I wanted to live, to be around to watch Andy grow up, and that there was always a chance that this might not happen. The deep feelings that flooded me were terribly moving. So, George, I can see your pain, and I'll have to support you here. It's probably better to

> keep your distance, or else you
> risk having to cope with all these
> deep feelings that you never lose
> and will have to live with.

(Tears welled up in Mrs. Combs' eyes; Mr. Combs appeared visibly moved.)

This early session with the Combs family served as a pivotal one in that there followed a marked change in the father-son relationship. Once George opened himself up to his son, the emotional exchange between him and his wife also seemed to benefit. In subsequent sessions, it became possible to examine the internalized myths of both parents which were responsible for rigidifying male-female role behavior and, in consequence, producing their strained relationship.

It was Mrs. Combs who initiated family therapy, complaining of an unsatisfying marriage, although she was unable to identify just what it was between them that was causing her to feel empty and discontented. Any effort to explore their relationship encouraged both partners to close up; while she became accusatory, George became silent and withdrawing. Patty was the pivot around which discussion was possible within limits. The play session pushed those limits by setting George up for a therapeutic bind. First, if he followed the instructions, he was cooperating with the writer—something he quite clearly did not intend to do; second, if he disobeyed the instructions and became closer to his son, he was also cooperating with the writer as the therapeutic objective was set in motion.

The strength of this strategy is its efficacy in generating some degree of movement by unhooking family members from their rigid patterns, ergo, setting the groundwork for more extensive exploration into the family myth structure.

STRATEGY IV: MODELING FOR CHANGE, CHILDREN'S RIGHTS

In the previous section, the focus of the Combs family interview evolved out of a play session between the writer and the family's 3-year old son, Patty.

It is not uncommon for a family to bring a young child into the weekly therapy sessions. The presence of a young child can often serve as a key toward unlocking rigid family patterns of raising a child. The child's presence offers an opportunity for a therapeutic strategy whereby the therapist engages in play and discussion with the youngster toward shaping new models of parenting and adult-child relations.

Interacting with a child can serve to challenge the social invention of "fatherhood" and move the male parent toward a comfortable androgyny that redefines male role behavior. If the marriage seems unfulfilling, a shift to the children frequently opens up more fruitful areas for growth and affection.

Operationally, it is good practice to make provision for a very young child by selecting play materials which are attractive and appropriate to the developmental level of the youngster.

In doing this, the child's needs are clearly taken into account; moreover, it affords an opportunity either to play with the youngster and/or engage in uninterrrupted conversation with the parents. Since many fathers simply will not or cannot engage in children's play before the youngster reaches an age where he or she can participate in adult activities, the play session provides an excellent therapeutic arena.

For this work the writer engaged children in a variety of play while both parents observed from the perimeter of the room. Play included drawing designs, figures followed by discussions based upon fantasy, magical thinking; shaping clay figures; using small dolls and creating dialogue between them; building with tinker toys, etc.

The presence of preadolescent and adolescent-aged youngsters in the therapy session provides a forum in which parents can be helped to take their youngsters' lives seriously. Attention is focused upon the plight of the teenager in this culture while examining the social forces responsible for many dilemmas young people endure.

Three areas seemed to stand out as troublespots and received greatest attention. The areas identified as most problematic by young people were: (a) school-related demands: (b) economics; and (c) peer group pressures.

Each of these problem areas was rooted into internalized parental myths embracing an overwhelming sense of duty and responsibility to govern the lives of their offspring. Despite the complexity of the social scene, the parents in this study felt obligated to monitor their children's development by enforcing patterns of dependency responsible for strain and hostility between themselves and their children.

Three beliefs attached to school, economics, and the peer group emerged in rigid forms requiring particular attention.

1. The child must go to school and conform to school standards which define the "appropriateness" of the youngster's growth, adjustment, and determine future success (a one-way affair.)
2. An allowance should take care of a youngster's needs. If a job is sought, it must assume secondary importance to school and home responsibilities.
3. Family values should supercede peer group values.

Each belief, although riddled with contradictions, was rigidly supported in one form or another. Resistance to an examination of the realities of a youngster's life is a rule of thumb in almost every family system. At the base of these beliefs was an overwhelming adherence to the idea that children, until they reach the age of 21, have no rights of their own. It followed that any serious attention paid to the aforementioned beliefs set the stage for change, particularly in the power-relations governing the family system. Granting the idea of children having their own lives and rights shifts the balance of power and responsibility from the parents to the child. Of course, each issue was positioned within a developmental framework, such as a child of five is *not* free to cross a large intersection simply because he or she desires to do so; and in such cases, the parents must exert their authority regarding activities which present clearly defined hazards to one's safety.

The hidden agenda serving as underlife to each of these issues is the structure of society, blatantly antichild in design. The socio-political consciousness-raising in this work is designed to raise the awareness of the parents to the fact that many tensions and hostilities generated between parents and children are spawned by virtue of the socio-cultural form rather than inherent in the parent-child interaction.

As an example of this issue, one family in therapy complained bitterly about the waxing hostility between the mother and her preschool-age daughter. The parent was simply distraught and terribly guilty over the discontentment she felt toward her child. Tearfully, she cited her deep feelings of guilt as unjust, for here she was, happily married, with a beautiful home, the daughter for whom she had wished, friends, no real financial stresses—she simply could not fathom the source of her growing discontent. Worse than that, her husband was furious with her since they had certainly acquired most, if not all, of their mutually shared myths and dreams.

As therapy progressed, it was not difficult to identify those factors which were influencing her to feel as she described.

1. The residential area was zoned for one acre per home. Not only were there few friends for her daughter, but mother had to transport her everywhere to see them.
2. There were few friends for the mother, forcing her to drive a considerable distance to be with her peers. More often than not, she had her daughter along and had to watch her constantly.
3. The shopping area required driving to reach it.
4. She disliked household chores and had been a real estate agent before having a baby.
5. Her husband was home in the late evening and the time they spent together was minimal; he did little parenting.
6. Her parents had recently retired and, as many retired couples do, they moved to Florida for the winter months.

Each of these issues was simply ignored, or the family was simply unaware of them, as they structured their lives to acquire the "Hollywood" setting that is presented as the "American Dream." Although many issues raised heretofore were amenable to solution, they were hidden beneath the growing hostility and depression felt by the mother, which she attributed to the on-going demands of her child. Their interaction when therapy first began was filled with tension. These parents lacked an understanding of the normal developmental stages of growth in children, and were ignorant of the connection to their circumstances. They had built their lives on the pursuit of the American Dream and could not fathom how it could be less than wonderful. It followed that it must be the child who is responsible for their disharmony.

It seemed as if these situations were common in family therapy settings. The inability to sort out issues by placing the burden of proof in the right direction all too often leads to a misplaced diagnosis. The need to raise consciousness to the socio-political issues lying at the hub of increasing family problems seemed justified and was brought into the therapy sessions.

In the above case, modeling was coupled with an examination of those underlife issues pregnant with myth that were responsible for maintaining the status quo. For this particular family, a decision was made by both parents to relocate their residence in a community reported to offer a much broader range of activities in which each family member could partake, not the least of which was a cooperative day-care center offering an opportunity for the mother to resume her vocation on a part-time basis. The improvement in general family relations was considerable.

STRATEGY V: STRUCTURING FAMILY CONFLICT

A fundamental problem in family therapy is that it lacks a taxonomy through which interpersonal problems can be described. Despite the shift away from treating symptoms from an intrapsychic perspective, family therapists still tend to rely upon diagnostic models which favor individual psychopathology.

In the absence of such a taxonomy, the writer has developed a tentative working model in order to conceptualize problems between individuals thus shifting from an intrapsychic to an interpersonal framework. This shift encourages the therapist to formulate treatment plans in accord with relationship problems.

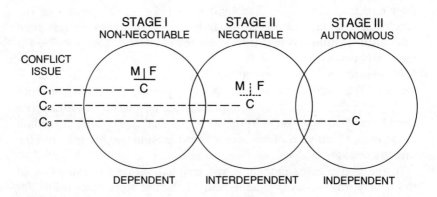

This model limits its scope to an analysis of interpersonal conflict. It identifies the conflict issue, the persons involved, and the stage where the conflict is positioned.

Stage I (Nonnegotiable) pertains to issues that are not subject to negotiation. Here, a relationship is dependent so that one family member regulates and controls another. For all intents and purposes, this is a relationship peculiar to a parent with a very young child. A child is told to do something and no discussion about it is invited.

Stage II (Negotiable) pertains to issues that are subject to negotiation. In this stage an issue involves an arrangement where mutual consent is required. Here, an interdependent relationship between two or more family members is flexible so that an issue is subject to modification and change mutually agreed upon by all parties concerned.

Stage III (Autonomous) pertains to issues that are not subject to any family member's opinion, involvement, or interference. As such, a person is independent and exercises his/her preference in a discretionary manner within limits self-imposed.

Discussion

In every family, each member finds issues that are positioned in all three stages. Commonly, a very young child is in a dependent relationship with his/her parent so that the majority of issues fall into stage I. When, however, a maturing child is unable to shift some issues from stage I to stages II and III, conflict develops. In such cases, the striving for independence is blocked by parental pressure pitted against increasing autonomy.

In other cases it is common to observe an adolescent who, in the process of gaining independence, demands that issues all fall into stage III. As such, a refusal to cooperate and negotiate with other family members sharpens the edge of conflict between him/herself and the family.

Finally, conflict between adults in a relationship can also be measured by using this model. Frequently, one partner, finding him/herself in stage I or III, strains the relationship sufficiently so that tensions and conflict abound. A family therapist diagramming issues between a couple can rapidly identify areas of disagreement and plan for a shift so that stage II predominates.

Since family therapy usually begins with an identified patient, it is useful to diagram this patient as early in treatment as possible.

Case Illustration

The Kornfeld Family—Craig, 14 years old (Identified Patient)

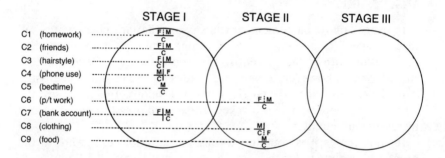

SESSION 3 IN FAMILY THERAPY: Craig Kornfeld (14)

> This diagram was completed after the third session with the Kornfeld
> family. A study indicates that many conflict areas involving Craig and his
> parents are positioned in either Stage I or Stage II. It is questionable as to
> whether any of these issues should be at Stage I with a fourteen-year old.
> Clearly, there is little mutuality involved in decision making.
> Therapeutically, it is important to set objectives toward shifting the
> balance of issues in Stages II and III. In the following interview, this
> objective is demonstrated.

Mark and Ellen Kornfeld entered family therapy at the recommendation of the school guidance counselor. Craig, their 14-year-old son,
had been constantly underachieving, despite comments listed on his
records citing high intelligence and above-average ranking on both
district-wide reading and mathematics examination.

At the initial meeting, the parents claimed to have experimented with a variety of methods in order to influence Craig toward improving his school work and attitude. They had appealed to reason, bribed, threatened, coerced, punished, and left him alone, all to no avail. The last report card listed failure in three out of four major subjects, with an unsatisfactory recorded in shop, typing, and physical education. He did manage to pass choral music.

As the writer introduced himself to the family, the evidence that Craig was an unwilling participant was overwhelming. He sat in the waiting room apart from the family facing the wall, an angry expression welling up on his face. When the family entered the therapy room, Craig quickly chose a seat away from everyone else, positioning it at right angles to his father; here, he could stare at the wall. Mr. and Mrs. Kornfeld sat facing one another and Michelle, their 10-year-old daughter, quietly seated herself between them, facing the writer.

Almost immediately, a raging argument erupted between Craig, who insisted he would not stay, and Marc, who warned him that he had better participate, since the choice was not his to make. They bantered back and forth and Craig was becoming more visibly upset. At this point, the writer requested all family members to wait in the outside room with the exception of Craig, who was asked to remain. For a brief moment, it seemed as though everyone was relieved, including Craig.

The writer then attempted to make a few comments in an effort to make contact with Craig. The one comment that broke the ice was when the writer acknowledged Craig's obvious resentment about coming for this session against his will (as can be seen in the following dialogue).

Craig
You're right . . . I don't want to be here . . . I have no problem.

An attempt is made to affiliate with Craig by accepting his resistance and then reframing the problem from that which his parents identify into one defining his struggle to refuse therapy.

Confusion in the writer's reply shifts Craig's attention to what is

Writer
I can see that the problem you're having now is that you are here against your will. I'm going to help you with that, because my work is helping families solve some of their problems, and the way I'm going to help you is that we'll tell your parents that you

said, following which the writer assumes command by paradoxically granting Craig permission to make his own decision.

are not to be here. I can't work with anyone who doesn't want to be here. There's no sense to it. Now your parents think they're here to solve the problem over your grades. What I'm going to do is to see them without you and solve their problem. I might include your sister, or I might not, but you can stay home . . . unless you decide to be here. In fact, here is my card with my phone number. You can always reach me here unless I'm not here, and if I'm not, I'll return your call when I get the message. But Craig, I'd prefer that you didn't call me for a while, because I must work with your parents about your grades and your not wanting to be here in these sessions, then I will see you.

Craig
Suppose I decide to come?

A double-bind tactic is used in order to reaffirm the writer's "in-charge" role by again granting permission to Craig to make his own decision.

Writer
I don't want you to decide until you're ready to. It's best not to rush . . . give me a few weeks just with your parents. Then you can decide, but I may not be able to see you unless we both agree.

Craig
When do you think I should come?

The writer exaggerates Craig's resistance.

Writer
I have work to do with your parents first. Don't rush. I want you to be sure, absolutely sure, when the time is best for you to come in. At this point, there is no sense to it since you don't want to be here. Now I want to use the rest of the time today with your parents. Remember, you can call me when you're ready. Also, if I see something happening that's very important, I'll call you. I'm not sure when that will be, but if I need you, will you be willing to come?

Craig
I don't know . . . maybe.

Again, Craig's indecisiveness is reframed so that the writer takes charge of it while validating the youngster's position. The writer then joins Craig in admitting his own doubts about progress.

Writer
Good. I don't want a definite answer, because I'm not sure myself. What time can I reach you where we can talk privately?

Craig
About 7 o'clock I'm home.

A further attempt is made to bind the idea that Craig and the writer will communicate in the near future.

Writer
Can we talk privately? . . . Sometimes it's difficult to carry on a private conversation when the whole family is around . . . you know what I mean.

The concept of privacy is underscored, affirming the position that Craig is a separate individual, entitled to private concerns.

Craig
I could go up to my parents' room and use the extension.

Writer
Good. In fact, when you call me, call me from there . . . O.K.?

Craig
Yeah . . . but I probably won't!

Writer
O.K. Take care, Craig, I'll see you soon.

The following session explores Mr. and Mrs. Kornfeld's relationship. There is a history of marital problems which is examined along with immediate issues involving Craig. Marc Kornfeld is an attorney, presently entangled with a number of financial setbacks in his practice.

One year ago, the Kornfelds made a bar mitzvah for Craig which cost them over $10,000—this was done despite pressing financial problems.

This conversation is a portion of the audiotape of session 3, dealing with the fact that Craig has not yet been involved in the therapeutic process, nor has any contact with him ensued since the first meeting.

Ellen
I want you to know that Craig asked when you are going to call him.

The writer acknowledges Craig's
right to make choices.

Writer
Oh, I'm glad to hear that. I did tell him that when he's ready he can call me and we'll get together.

Ellen
I doubt if he'll do that . . . I don't want to wait too long or he'll lose interest.

Writer
That could be true . . . but, on the other hand, people often want what they can't easily get.

Marc (laughs)
That's true.

Writer
Look how anxious the two of you are about Craig's grades.

While grades are often used as a measure of unsuccessful parenting, Marc directs his concerns toward his son's irresponsible attitude. He implicates neither the school nor himself for Craig's behavior. He does not see Craig's behavior as a way of extricating himself from the wedge; on one side stands the school, and on the other, he and Ellen. For Marc, it is Craig who must make the first move.

Marc
It's not the grades . . . it's his effort. He makes no effort. He's lazy and irresponsible and that's what eats the shit out of me. All his teachers have told me how bright he is and how much better he could do if he put in a little work. But Craig, forget it . . . he'd rather sit on his ass and watch TV, or nag me to take him somewhere or do something for him. To get him to do a little work is impossible. That's all he needs, a little effort, and the teachers would give him passing grades. You think he cares? He does absolutely nothing . . . If he would try and fail, I'd accept it. But to do nothing and then to expect the world to cater to him . . . to me, that's bullshit. That's all I ask out of him . . . !

Writer (turning to Ellen)
What do you think?

While Craig precipitates much tension between them, he also offers them a point of reference out of which some mutuality is achieved. Problems between them are shelved as Craig de-

Ellen
Marc is right. He never does his homework and if I ask him to go to the store . . . or a, take out the garbage . . . I get an argument. He never does it willingly.

flects and absorbs the differences in their relationship.

Marc
That's what I mean . . . he refuses to take responsibility . . . just demands, that's what he's good at . . . and if you say no, he nags and nags and wears you down. He can't take no for an answer. He'll scream and nag until I have to rap him. . . . That's the only thing that shuts him up.

Writer
He really can frustrate the hell out of you.

Marc explains his relationship with Craig in extremes; either he becomes overinvolved and authoritarian, or he reaches for maximum distance.

Marc
I'm sick and tired of getting on his back, but if you leave him alone he does nothing. He doesn't give a damn. He's spoiled rotten. Whatever the hell he wants, he gets . . . but you get nothing back from him. . . . No more. Nothing but aggravation. I've had it with him!

The bar mitzvah is one of many institutions that burden the family with social pressure. There, the parents transform their social requirements onto Craig, who is expected to conform to the expectations crossing cultural, family, and community lines.

Writer
That was one hellova affair you made for his bar mitzvah last year. Did he appreciate it?

Marc
Are you kidding? Ten thousand bucks and I had to be on his back right up to the last minute or else he wouldn't have learned his *haftorah*. Even that was aggravation.

Neither Marc nor Ellen has been active in Jewish community life or the temple.

The rigid posture with regard to maintaining images involves having Craig conform to the social rituals. The fact that they borrowed money for his bar mitzvah is enough to expect that he appreciate it in a manner that pleases them. That Craig may have felt guilty and angry over this has not been considered.

Ellen
He took the heart out of it . . . right to the last minute.

Marc
Like I said . . . do you think he appreciated it? Forget it. It's like it never happened. A day later, he was exactly the same. No thank you . . . nothing!

Ellen
That's true. Not a word of thanks!

Writer
It's just amazing how much we do for our kids and they just don't seem to appreciate it. It can really eat your *kishkas* out! My friends made a wedding like that for their daughter . . . even though she said she didn't want it . . . You know, a big lavish affair, and the next day it was like it never happened. Were they disheartened! She wanted a little ceremony with a few close friends and relatives . . . but you know how it is . . . we get so caught up in making these things for people . . . like business associates and distant relatives. This friend of mine actually took a loan . . . can you imagine? . . . for a wedding his daughter didn't want . . . It's enough to really eat your heart out . . . and, once it's over, it's like a fantasy, a bad dream . . . Here his daughter begged him not to do it, but this

guy, he's like a mule. [laughter] He needed it and there was no stopping him. . . . And after it was over, his daughter and son-in-law moved to the West Coast and now they hardly speak to one another. . . . But what can you do, right?

Ellen
Craig didn't want a big bar mitzvah.

Marc encouraged Craig to invite many friends without setting limits. He criticizes Craig for being irresponsible, but encourages nothing less from him.

Marc
He was having a damn good time when I looked at him. Do you know that this kid invited over 30 friends . . . you know what that cost me?

Writer
I can imagine. And with all the other guests . . . you told me, Marc . . . over ten thousand dollars. That's a lot of money. Just living on a daily basis is expensive as hell. Why, when I go into a supermarket I can hardly believe my eyes. Last week it cost me $16.00 for a few items . . . I tell you, I really appreciate what my wife keeps telling me about the sky-rocketing cost of foods. Just amazing!

Monetary issues have been a bone of contention between Ellen and Marc.

Ellen
You should do the weekly shopping for a family of four . . . I can't get away with under $80.00 every time I walk into the store

... and Marc thinks I'm not careful enough!

Marc's concern for bargains flies in the face of his extravagance when it suits his needs.

Marc
I didn't say that ... But she doesn't look for bargains ... that's what annoys me. She takes the first item she sees.

Ellen
I told you ... when you're ready to do the shopping it's fine with me, otherwise don't complain.

Writer
It seems like no matter how much we earn, it's still not enough for what we want to do.

Marc
Would you believe that I'm 41 years old, make a damn good income, and I still have to count pennies. I can't even go on a decent vacation this summer! Craig has to go to summer school and we're short of money. It's the same bullshit and I'm tired of it. I can never creep out of the hole.

Writer
You figure that by this time in your life, you shouldn't have to be struggling.

The spiraling money crunch is a strong source of anger and tension. He resents the constraints

Marc
Damn right ... and all you get for it is a kick in the teeth. She

that he believes he should not have based upon the salary he earns. Interestingly, Ellen handles the bills, so Marc really has a rather childish understanding of how and where their money is allocated. To him, the salary he makes weekly seems impressive, and yet his desire to be self-indulgent has been limited. Ellen is an easy target to blame.

nags me . . . gets on Craig's back . . . he's not doing his work. Goddamn it, it's his problem . . . who needs this shit! You bust your ass in business . . . come home figuring your home is the place to unwind, relax, do what you want, and everybody needs something else that you should do for them . . . Two fuckin' weeks off this summer, and she tells me we don't have the money to take a place in the Hamptons. What the fuck is that? . . . You wonder why so many couples are in splitsville . . . half our friends are split and the other half are fuckin' around. . . .

Writer
We build a dream, a fantasy, and we get ourselves caught inside.

Marc
You bet. If I want to take time for myself, she complains I'm neglecting her. Or the kids bitch that I don't take them anywhere.

The writer alludes to the social pressure behind the making of the bar mitzvah.

Writer
And you get stuck into making ten thousand-dollar affairs because you think that you have to, and there goes the money you both might have used for other things.

Now Ellen is certain that the bar mitzvah was made for her husband.

Ellen
Oh come on! That was his idea.

band. She has not accepted her own role in it, citing that she would have been satisfied with a less elaborate affair.

. . . I needed it like a hole in the head! I begged him to make a smaller one, but no, he had to impress everyone who we see from one year to the next . . . and for what? So he should look good. Right? Didn't I beg you to make a small party?

Marc is not about to let her get free of that without implicating her as well.

Marc
You said it . . . but don't tell me you didn't want the whole thing . . . as much or more than me. Now you turn around and make me look like the one who wanted it . . . Bullshit!

Writer
How did you know Ellen wanted it just as much as you did?

Marc identifies the pressure he believes Ellen places upon him in subtle ways.

Marc
Are you kidding, Doc? She loves to look good . . . just as concerned with other people's opinions, maybe more than me. She tells you she wanted a small affair . . . but she reminds me a thousand times of her friends' affairs . . . Miss simple here! How many times have you told me that this friend went to Europe and this one just bought a new car . . . Come on now . . . Let's call a spade a spade!

The writer reframes Marc's response to this "pressure" as caring for Ellen and choosing to please her.

Writer
You certainly care about pleasing Ellen.

Ellen
Oh, come off it! He pleases himself!

Writer
Somebody's got wires crossed
here.

Marc
I need an electrician. [laughter]

Writer
I bet Craig doesn't realize how
much you're pleasing him either.
[laughter]
People . . . I think maybe we are
ready to bring Craig in and con-
vince him just how much everyone is pleasing one another, but
doesn't seem to realize it!
[laughter]

In fact, Marc and Ellen do try to
please each other, although it
does not come out that way in
the end.

I think you can tell he and
Michelle that I'm ready to see
them because some important
things have come up and now I
need them to help me here.

Ellen
Good luck! [laughter] We'll see
you next week.

Writer
Have a good week . . . and keep
pleasing one another! [laughter
and hand-shaking]

(The following is a portion of the audiotape recorded during the fourth
session with the Kornfeld family. Both Michelle and Craig attended
after the parents informed them that they had been invited by me.
Surprisingly, Craig offered little resistance to this.)

Greeting all members and then quickly shifting into the topic of the weather was a result of the writer's discernment that considerable tension and anger were in the prevailing mood.

Writer
Ah, come in, come in people. Marc [handshake], Ellen, Craig [shoulder tap] and Michelle [handshake] . . . What a miserable day! Did you have any difficulty driving over in this downpour?

Ellen
To tell you the truth, we almost canceled at the last minute. I hate driving in a heavy rain. I get very nervous.

The weather was a safe topic with which to make contact with Michelle, thereby affiliating with her and dispelling some of the tension. The writer was also aware that once the session began, Michelle would have a relatively inactive role.

Writer
I'm glad you all came. Actually, I heard that it's supposed to blow over. Maybe by the time you leave the storm will pass, or at least ease up a bit. What do you think, Michelle, do you think the storm will ease up so that your family can travel home easier, and mother can relax?

Michelle [shrugging her shoulders]
I don't know . . . [smiles shyly]

The writer comments metaphorically on family life, then shifts to Craig, citing how well he seems to look. This was an attempt to disarm some of his anger about being part of the session. A comment acknowledging that Craig came on his own reframes his anger about being part of the session.

Writer
Well, some storms we can't control and others maybe we can do something about. Craig, I haven't seen you for quite some time . . . if looks tell the truth, you're really doing great! I'm glad you decided to come in tonight . . . As I said to you, as soon as things change, or some-

thing came up where I needed
you, Id let you know. It's good
that you're here. Your mom,
dad, and I covered a lot of
ground . . . and maybe got a few
things straightened out between
them. But, as I told you, family
problems often require everyone's presence. . . . Anyway,
how have things been?

Craig [staring off to the side]
Pretty much the same.

Writer
Which means?

Craig
Nothing's really changed.

Writer
Michelle?

Michelle
Uh, well, maybe a little better.

Writer
Like how?

Less overt conflict does not necessarily mean better relationships. The writer decides to
bring that to everyone's attention.

Michelle
Maybe a little less fighting . . .
my mother and father are arguing less.

Writer
Is that good for the family?

Michelle
Uh-huh. [chuckles] It's quieter.

Writer
I bet it's wonderful to have some peace and quiet for a while.

Michelle
Uh-huh. I like it.

Again, the idea of peace and quiet as always good is raised for questioning.

Writer
Of course, too much of it . . . peace and quiet . . . is also tough to take?

Marc, anxious for a confrontation, shifts the direction of the dialogue by positioning Craig as the problem. He comes right in with a provocative issue in order to demonstrate just how difficult Craig is.

Marc
Craig, why don't you tell Dr. Solomon about the note your science teacher sent home? [Silence]

Writer
Oh boy! I bet dad just pushed the button on peace and quiet!

Marc
Craig . . . tell him what the note said!

Craig
You tell him, O.K.!?

Marc
His science teacher informed us that unless he hands in six assignments, he will definitely fail for the period. Do you think that bothers him? He does absolutely nothing about it . . . nothing . . .

Craig
I told you not to write him a letter.

Marc

The fact that he's failing science doesn't bother him . . . my letter bothers him. I told Craig, and Ellen will bear me out, that I will stop writing letters when he shows me some effort. He doesn't open a book. Not once this week did he open a book, even though he knew a test was coming up on Friday.

Craig

I told you not to write a letter and not to go up to see my teacher . . . that's all!

Marc

This is what I get from him all the time . . . no matter what it is! I told him I'll do what I think is best until he shows me something. When I want to see your teachers I'll see them! When you do what's expected of you, then I'll have no reason to see them.

Craig

You'll still see them. You always say that, but you never keep your promise . . . never . . . you lie all the time!

Marc

I'll keep mine when you do what you're supposed to . . . You never open a book. When I study with him, he doesn't listen to a thing I say, except what he wants to hear . . . I'm sick and tired of your temper tantrums and your irresponsible ways!

The writer reframes Marc's intrusiveness as a way of caring for his son.

Writer
I can see how much you care about your son. That's pretty clear to me . . . and how much you want him to do the right thing.

Marc
He does nothing but demand, demand, on everybody . . . What does he give back—can you tell me that? Nobody asks him to do a goddamn thing except take care of his own responsibilities . . . in school . . . and once in a while around the house a little. That's it! The boy gets everything he needs! Appreciate it. . . . Forget it!

Craig
I appreciate it . . . what do you want from me!

[Father repeats the same, adding specific household chores that Craig fails to do.]

Writer
You know, one of the differences between a parent's pressures and a kid's pressures is that a parent, no matter how frustrated or grudgingly he feels about the load he carries, at least he believes it's useful or needed in one way or another.

Marc
What do you mean?

The writer affiliates with the father by admitting that both he and the writer do things for the family in a dutiful way—which sometimes brings a sense of gratification, despite the demands and frustrations.

Writer
I guess I wasn't clear. Well, take yourself, or me for an example. We both keep long hours . . . work hard . . . often give up certain things we want to do for the family. But even though there's resentment about doing it, at least at times we still feel we are doing something important . . . maybe even heroic . . . you know what I'm driving at? [Marc listens attentively]

The writer alludes to the power that grades and school performance hold in setting up standards for evaluating a youngster's self-worth; beyond school, many children feel valueless to their families.

But kids . . . well, many of them, at least nowadays, get the impression that, ah, nothing they really do makes all that much difference. Now correct me if I'm wrong . . . but unless a kid is very interested in school work—which some kids are and, admittedly this makes life much easier for their parents—a lot of kids feel like they're excess family baggage, so to speak. It's strange, but I think many kids today often feel as if nothing they do matters that much!

Marc's caring side has been reached. There's a sense of pride as he mentions that Craig does not settle easily for things. He seems to feel an affiliation with his son at this point.

Marc
Well, Ellen and I have tried to tell Craig how important his school grades are for later . . . if he wants to make something of himself. I've tried to tell him that it's a tough world out there

. . . unless you're well prepared you're gonna find yourself in a bad situation. He's not a kid who settles for things . . . right, Craig? He likes expensive stereos, bicycles, vacations . . . how the hell does he get that without preparing himself? Maybe we provide these things for him now, but later, who's going to foot the bills? Eighteen, and he's on his own. I'll pay for school, but that's it, and I won't pay if he thinks he's going on a vacation. Anything else, he's on his own.

The writer acknowledges the father's role, then suggests that Craig's needs have been acquired by the family lifestyle. The writer quickly introduces the idea that we are victims of social forces, and that even by following the prescribed route (school) there are no surefire guarantees of financial success.

Writer
Well, there's no argument with that. You want Craig to understand the importance school will have for him, and how he can't buy the kinds of things he has been taught to need. I know what you mean, Marc. We've been brought up on a diet of TV, stereos, two cars, $10,000 weddings—it's pretty tough not to expect that our kids will also be victims of the commercial marketplace . . . and I know that you want to prepare him for this . . . so he gets what he wants . . . earns the money to pay for it . . . not that going to college guarantees a high income—

Marc
That's true . . .

For the first time Craig is presented in a favorable light.

Rather than permit Marc to pursue his line of thought, the writer again reframes the father's criticism into something that the family accepts as a value for them.

The writer furthers the observation—"like father like son." The humor allows Marc to admit the similarity without feeling threatened.

Ellen
Craig, tell Dr. Solomon how you earned money . . . on the paper route . . . He did so well, he bought his own speakers for the stereo. Tell him about that, Craig.

Marc
When he wants to do something, he does it. No question about it. If it's for him, he'll do the job. If it's for someone else . . . forget it, unless he feels like it.

Writer
I know it may sound crazy, but, the two of you have really done a fine job . . . in preparing him for the road ahead. Admittedly—correct me if I'm wrong—you both live high. And it seems to me, Craig has learned that lesson pretty well. [laughter] You've got a good pragmatic attitude, Marc, and I can see how you want Craig to become a hard-headed realist. Yes . . . I can say he's on his way!

Marc [laughter]
You mean we spoiled him good!

Writer
Well, I didn't say spoiled. I said you've given him a taste of what you consider the good life. Unfortunately, he's too young to go

out and take care of himself. School demands he delay . . . and, since school doesn't bring immediate rewards, it is harder for Craig to discipline himself for the long run. In the meantime, you are the one who's pressured to provide the immediate reward. . . . Years ago, kids were out working and contributing to the family as young as 12; now they're expected in some cases to remain in school—kind of an extended adolescence—until they're into their mid-twenties, and in some cases beyond that. If a kid is not really attached to learning, at least as it is presented in school, it's a real problem. In many cases, that's the primary place where they get recognition. And if it doesn't come there . . . where then?

Marc
You've got a point there!

Craig is again mentioned in a favorable light. There is an attempt to link our attitude about school to so many other concerns regarding the conduct of our children. Moreover, our criticism increases the estrangement between ourselves and our offspring as this pattern becomes circular with no resolution.

Writer
It's a real problem with a kid like Craig. Nothing much more is expected of him than eating and dressing himself and going to school . . . to do well. If that's not working, parents find themselves in a situation where they're constantly criticizing, since so much of what a kid is measured by grades, and a few household jobs . . . Right? . . . When grades are poor, we often

begin criticizing their friends, the way they spend leisure time, and all sorts of other things . . . Or we think it's a reflection of our parenting.

Marc
What else can we do?

Writer
Well, the more we criticize, the angrier and more resentful our kid becomes, and the less willing he is to please or respond; then we become increasingly more frustrated. It goes around and around.

Ellen
That's true, and nothing gets better, either.

The writer now draws an analogy to business, since Marc is currently having similar difficulties.

Writer
It's like business. If it declines, it affects our attitude about so many related things. If it gets better, we increase our expenses in order to expand; you take in more work, then that requires additional help and more hours . . . and soon you find yourself no better off than when you started. [Marc nods his head affirmatively] Unless you find an optimal point, you keep increasing your efforts with no real returns.

Marc
It's the same in the way we live!

I had a good year, what do you think we did! We sold our house and bought one that cost a helluva lot more. You think it's better?

Ellen
Marc, you know we both like it more than our other house . . .

Marc
Yeah, but the increased monthly payments and the insane taxes . . . we coulda used the money to do other things.

Respecting and acknowledging the children as important people in the family is now introduced. A move is often difficult for them.

Writer
And I bet, like most of us, you barely consulted the kids about the move at all.

Marc
What do they know? [Laughs]

Writer
They know if they are happy or satisfied with where they are living . . . a move forces them to find new friends . . . leave old and familiar friends, community—along with many other difficult adjustments not often obvious to us.

Michelle comes forward on this one.

Michelle
That's true, Daddy . . . I still like it in our other house better.

Marc
Don't you like it where we live now?

Michelle
Uh huh, but I miss my friends
. . . and I liked my old school a
little better.

Craig
You never said one word to us
. . . we're moving, that's all.
You think I wanted to move? I
hate it here. But you and
Mommy wanted a bigger house,
so now we have one. So what!
You never asked me nothing!

Marc
Why didn't you say anything
then?

Changing their residence was a
decidedly emotional issue for
both children. It was one of the
few that Michelle spoke to during the session.

Craig
You never listen to us . . .
never! You're always busy doing
something else . . . or criticizing.
Whatever I do you criticize . . .
and I hate it! You're always on
my back. You put down my
friends, my clothes, my hair . . .
Every week—Craig, when you
gonna get a haircut? . . . All you
know how to do is put us down.
. . . You think you're the greatest!

Ellen
Craig!

Craig
Forget it! Just forget it!

Marc
Finish what you were saying . . .
come on . . .

Craig
If you get off my back—and Mom, if she stops nagging, nagging—maybe I'd do better.

Marc
That's a first class cop-out. We weren't on your back a whole semester. What did you get? You failed three majors and gym . . . gym! Could you believe the athlete here failed gym!

Craig
You said school is my problem . . . and then you and Mommy get on my back!

Marc
It's your problem, but when you fail it's my problem. Start doing your work and I'll leave you alone.

Craig
I didn't say leave me alone. I said get off my back . . . stop criticizing me, that's all! Stop nagging me all the time!

A distinction between being left alone (abandoned) as contrasted to having freedom to make some of one's own decisions is an important one to examine here. Craig wanted the latter, but he also wanted attention from his parents.

Writer
While you complained about being nagged, Marc, I don't think you meant being left alone as an alternative, did you?

Marc
Well . . . sometimes I want Ellen to be around . . . to be with me, like if we're working together on say the lawn or

something, and . . . we both enjoy it.

Writer
Then there's no nagging?

Marc
No . . . that's not nagging. Nagging is when Ellen keeps telling me to do something over and over again when I don't feel like doing it. Or she insists that it's got to be done her way . . . and she'll repeat it 100 times until I either walk out or we have a fight.

Craig
That's what you do to me, Dad . . . all the time . . . every time I ask you to help me with my homework you're on my back, nagging me and criticizing me. And I tell you to stop and you get mad.

Marc
I get mad because you don't listen. You ask me to help and as soon as I tell you one thing you don't like, that's it.

Craig
You keep saying the same thing over and over.

Marc
Because you don't listen.

Craig
I listen. *You* don't listen! You never do. You're always saying: "you're wrong." I'm never right. Whatever I do, you say something to put me down.

Marc
I say something because I see you're doing something one way, and I think I know another way. In my opinion, a better way.

Craig
Always a better way! If I knock a nail in this way, you tell me that way.

Writer
You would like Dad to acknowledge that you can do quite a few things well, and on your own.

Craig
He never does . . . always a criticism, and I hate it! I really hate it. It makes me so mad!

Writer
Sometimes, even if a person has an opinion about how to do something, it's best they keep it to themselves . . . unless they are asked.

Craig
If I feel like doing some things my way, why does he always have to say something?

Writer

Parents like to help make their kids perfect . . . and even when criticism is given with good intentions, it's hard to take. People have a lot of trouble accepting criticism—from anyone.

Marc

Why can't he ever listen to what I'm telling him without throwing a fit or walking away?

Arguing about who is right or wrong often masks a struggle for power in relationships. Many family arguments actually contain no right-wrong positions, though they are fought as if they did.

Writer

Well, it seems to me that we all need some space to do things in our own way—even if mistakes are being made—and sometimes we learn by the errors we make, hopefully at least. But more important—and you gave a beautiful example when you spoke about yourself and Ellen in the garden—there are times that you just feel like having the freedom to do certain things just the way you like them to be. I mean, certain issues have no real right or wrong at all! . . . What comes into my mind is—for example, you want to plant the flowers on the right, and it seems right to you; and Ellen, she wants it on the left. And you argue about it as if there really were a right or wrong to it . . . while what the argument is really about is who will have the power to make the decision—or who will get their way. Right and wrong really have little or nothing to do with the whole thing.

Marc
That's very true. I like that idea. It's a good way to put it.

Writer
So many of these power tactics have been influenced by outside forces which we tend to accept as standards . . . unquestioned rules. We make them inflexible as a result of our willingness to accept them . . .

Marc
Yeah . . .

Writer
. . . and these rules so often get in the way of—how could I say—our own personal freedom. A good example of this has to do with raising children. Our kids grow older and want more space for making their own decisions about certain things that are important to them. I shouldn't say kids, because it's true for all of us. And one of the hardest places for this to happen is inside our family . . . because people live together and spend so much close time together we interfere in even the smallest details of other family members. Resentment builds.

Marc
That's what happens . . . you get on each other's back.

The idea of rigid patterns leading to arguments is introduced.
Family behavior establishes sets
of expectations which define individual conduct. If a family is
rigid, the slightest deviation sets
off trouble.

Writer
And then trouble starts! Look, in every family there are certain things that must get done. No question about it. And one per-son or another winds up doing a job . . . it just happens that way . . . and the rest of the family starts to expect or depend on that member to do what they were doing. Then there are things that people do together, they trade-off you might say, negotiate . . . and then there has to be some area where a person does basically as he chooses. The way he wants to . . . no ifs, ands, or buts . . . no interference . . . and everyone in the family needs to experience all three areas. For example: if someone wants to do something her way . . . she doesn't want interference—like planting a flower to the right, or doing a math problem—she needs the space to do it. Granted it's always easier to talk about this than to do it.

Ellen
It's worth a try, right, Craig?

Craig
It won't work!

Marc
See what I mean? Already he's downgrading an idea . . . even before we do anything.

The writer affirms Craig's skepticism since it expresses a truth about change: that it is very difficult to induce.

Writer
Well, maybe Craig is right. The problem with setting up rules or ways to behave . . . expectations . . . is that we're often disappointed because they don't work. In fact, the more you expect this to work, the more pressure you will be putting on one another and bang! You're back where you started. Actually, if you think about it, it's the expectations we have about one another that get us into trouble to begin with. Michelle, you've been very quiet. Does any of this stuff make sense to you?

Michelle
I don't really understand it—but, it sounds O.K. . . . .
[Laughter]

Writer
I can tell you, Michelle . . . if anyone here can put this to work, it's probably you!
[Laughter]

Family therapy with the Kornfelds was discontinued after fourteen sessions. The decision was unanimously arrived at since relationships were measurably improved. While Marc and Ellen still had areas of disagreement between them, they no longer involved Craig in a triangle, and instead confronted one another directly.

Craig evidenced a much greater degree of motivation to achieve at school. The difficulty with putting this into effect had to do with his disorganized approach to study. Craig's daily notebook resembled a sketch pad. There was simply no continuity evident as he lacked the skills necessary to record class notes in any systematic fashion.

This is a common problem that many youngsters encounter, particularly those who have done rather poorly at school for a prolonged period of time. To address this, the writer offered Craig an opportunity of working directly upon developing study skills. Since our rapport was favorable at this time, Craig expressed an interest which both Marc and Ellen were willing to support.

Five individual sessions with Craig were held with the expressed purpose of working on his approach to learning. For each session Craig was instructed to bring in all his books and we would then develop a method to enable him to use his intelligence and energy in the most efficient manner possible. The writer demonstrated techniques for careful note-taking, outlining book and research reports, reading a text for specific and general ideas, and preparing for various types of examinations. Each session began with Craig reciting that which was occurring in each class. The writer observed as homework was completed and would suggest different approaches to it. Craig worked enthusiastically and his attitude about school changed sharply.

Once a youngster develops a systematic approach to learning, it becomes habitual, much the same as any repeated pattern of behavior. While therapy can often generate a resurgence of enthusiasm, it cannot supply the tools through which a youngster can achieve. If this is neglected, what often happens is that in a short time school failure repeats itself. To this, it is important that the therapist either work with the youngster directly on his/her school work, or make an appropriate referral.

It is important to add that after three months Craig received a report card with fine grades. Marc was so pleased with this that the relationship between him and his son markedly improved. An additional session was held at this point in an effort to assess the changes that had occurred. While things seemed to be continuing along an even keel, both parents expressed some concern that Michelle's school achievement had fallen slightly. It was evident that some of the energy they directed toward Craig was now transferred to their daughter. Some time was devoted to discussing this, though no further sessions were immediately planned as a response to it. Whether this shift will work favorably is undeterminable at this writing. Suffice it to say, it is the writer's opinion that while Michelle will indeed become more visible now that Craig has extricated himself from the scapegoat role, her visibility need not duplicate the triangulation evident at the beginning of therapy. Only time will tell whether this remains true.

PROBLEMS AND PARADOXES OF TERMINATING THERAPY

The termination phase of family therapy poses its own unique problems, the principal one being the nature of the group itself. Other groups create an identity after therapy has begun, but the family unit brings to therapy complex, tangled relationships where the problems to be solved are a sequel of its own unique history.

At the first meeting, it is unusual to find all family members equally interested or willing to partake in the process. Considerable resistance may be voiced by one or more members strenuously objecting to a forced participation against their will.

During treatment, a commitment to continue the process fluctuates for each family member according to the changing focus of the sessions. It is rare when all concerned are simultaneously pleased with the issues under discussion or the direction in which therapy seems to be going.

The termination phase is the tail end, so to speak, the winding-down period after which therapy is discontinued. Reaching total client agreement in order to accomplish this is a decidedly difficult task and merits separate attention. The writer has, therefore, identified the following problems and paradoxes which complicate the termination of a family in therapy:

1. Terminating family therapy is frequently influenced by the therapist's assessment, a most prominent feeling of which is disappointment with the degree of change evident in the family, or in one or more of its members, prompting the family to remain in treatment.

When a therapist expresses this disappointment, the disclosure is a technique under the guise of a peremptory function. The therapist is aware of this, but the family is not.

It is admirable to uncover and examine the techniques openly. However, by alerting the clients to guard against the technique, the family is still being manipulated to remain in therapy. The inescapable paradox is that authenticity and honesty are both techniques which, despite forthright intention, produce a predictable response where one party is aware (of manipulation) and the other is not. In this instance the response refers to the double-binding nature of a therapist's disclosure: "It's all right if you, the family, decide to terminate but I, as your therapist, am not really pleased with the results thus far." At this point, it is recommended that the double-bind be exposed, with an explanation clarifying the coercive force governing unequal power relationships. Only then can a clearer decision be made.

2. Occasionally, one family member desires to continue in therapy after the group, as a whole, has decided to terminate. This can lead to problems, and the first concerns repercussions which follow the behavioral change.

While the family unit is cojointly participating in therapy, behavioral change is modulated through a homeostatic process regulating the family system—maintaining a pattern equilibrium establishing the controlling force which governs the interactions and interrelationships. Each individual's behavor, then, is responsive in kind to any and all changes occurring in one or more of its members. However, when one member elects to continue therapy alone, any change in that individual may seem precipitous and threatening to the family system and may result in the family as a whole returning to therapy.

As this struggle evolves it is an expression of the paradox of liberating an individual while conserving the integrity of the family unit. Within the struggle is the implicit assumption that change must lead to the dissolution of the family, unless it is orchestrated by all the players. Put another way, what may seem good for an individual is not necessarily good for a group relationship.

Indeed, there is a risk involved, and it is the responsibility of the therapist to acknowledge it. Perhaps no other issue in a relationship generates as much resistance as this one invariably does. Even where a relationship appears to be open or unrestrictive in the broadest terms, implicit forces are at work which maintain a steady-state balance. Subtle though they may be, these forces inhibit or discourage certain behavior, which, if exercised, automatically raises anxiety.

It is the therapist's responsibility to increase the elasticity of a relationship to the point where all parties concerned enjoy an optimum level of safety, security, and freedom. The integrity of a relationship can be preserved only when people understand that liberation and change require a tension that is supplied by constraint; that change can be inhibiting when it is pursued as an end in itself. Therefore, it is important to identify those issues which are influencing one member of the family to pursue therapy after the rest of the family is prepared to terminate.

This action, then, will discourage termination and instead invite the family to further the search for new boundaries.

Does this mean that an individual should be discouraged from continuing therapy after family therapy has ended? On the contrary, it is the family that should be encouraged to continue until a point is reached where they can support any member's request for same. And, as strange as it may seem, when that point is reached, the desire for individual therapy often becomes measurably less important.

The second issue pertains to economics. The fee for therapy is often high and in many instances burdens a family budget. In crises the money spent for therapy is viewed as a necessary and willing expense. As the situation improves, to the degree that a sense of urgency no longer exists, the fee for continuing therapy may be grudgingly paid. This is a common experience when one family member wishes to continue treatment after the most urgent problems have been ameliorated.

Often, a begrudging attitude on the part of the wage earner to continue the financial support of another family member in therapy is conceived as a sign of resistance to any further change. While in certain cases this may indeed be true, in other cases it is patently false. Paying for therapy taxes a family budget and cannot be summarily dismissed as a resistance to change. Instead, economics is an issue worthy of separate consideration. The controlling and dispensing of money is often central to related tensions that translate into other problems. Of course, the decision to examine further the issue of economics necessarily maintains the family in therapy and this must be clearly acknowledged.

3. The predetermined goal of symptom reduction in classic modes of symptom-oriented therapy will automatically cue the point of termination.

In other forms of therapy, termination is less definite and is reached when all concerned participants agree that the time has come to end. As a general consideration, it is admissible to entertain terminating therapy when things are judged to have improved, though traces of conflict remain.

There is a principle governing this notion conceived as "optimizing rather than maximizing" an experience. Farson (1978) discusses this in the framework of an idea that more of something does not necessarily mean improving upon it. He writes: "Implicit is the idea that the more congruence the better, the more openness the better, the more intimacy the better, and so forth. The more the better rather than one can get too much of a good thing—linear rather than curvilinear, maximizing rather than optimizing . . . not every itch should be scratched, even if our body is inclined to do so. It is positively dangerous to do so . . ." (p. 19.)

The urge to continue therapy is compelling when change has occurred. It is not difficult to influence a family to remain in therapy when they are pleased with the progress, but there is an inherent danger that they will become entrapped by newly created expectations, most notably the obsessive striving for more improvement as a response to increasing effort, as though doing more assures windfall results. A common enough experience, it is forgotten that maximizing effort can evoke the law of diminishing returns—an economic derivative.

It is advisable to consider terminating therapy before a number of distinct problems have been put to rest. This does not mean that, despite protestations to the contrary, a therapist willfully abandons a family. Instead, the idea refers to a notion that not all human problems readily yield to solutions, particularly when they are addressed through therapeutic intervention. A therapist might introduce the idea of termination based upon a recognition that the family has already sharpened their approach to conflict solving and in time will probably come to terms with problematic issues as they emerge.

A fuller understanding of this concept derives from the work of Ivan Illich, social philosopher and critic, who reintroduced the term "iatrogenesis" to explain how some problems may worsen by eager attempts to solve them. Using medicine as an example, Illich posits that in too many cases, the cure for an illness is worse than the disease it was designed to remedy.

It can be observed that not every problem in a relationship context can or should be ameliorated. In fact, working on solving some problems adds considerable strain to a relationship and may result in the rupturing of the bonds that maintain homogeneity.

Contrary to popular notion, it is often wise to make no intervention in certain problems. While taking no direct action may be thought of as irresponsible or neglectful, in plain fact, choosing not to do something is indeed an action in its own right.

This idea is particularly valuable to present to a family in therapy because it enlarges their understanding of problem solving while reducing the expectations they may harbor that either in or out of therapy all people-problems can be solved.

From this vantage point, a new way of considering a schedule for therapy evolves.

4. There is little reason to assume that family therapy, or for that matter therapy in general, must conform to a structured preset schedule. Typically, traditional therapy is scheduled on a weekly basis, though newer forms vary and in some cases include prolonged sessions held over a weekend or more.

Family therapy may be most effective when it conforms to the nature of a family problem, moreover to the style of life peculiar to the family system. For example, in some cases it may be wise to consider family meetings for one or two sessions, and then not schedule the next appointment for a month or more, allowing time for the family itself to put into use what it has learned. In other cases, the schedule can be arranged on short notice, thus conforming to emergent issues in a flexible and spontaneous manner.

The frequency and lengths of sessions can be planned according to the problem and, in many cases, this requires a departure from common form, which generally means weekly meetings. Eventually, the sessions will be spaced further apart.

5. There is no best way to terminate therapy. Granted there are premature terminations with unfortunate consequences; however, deciding upon a best or uniform procedure for concluding treatment intrusively narrows the expression of uniqueness and resiliency common to all relationships. For some, a short good-bye serves the same purpose as a prolonged embrace.

Problems emerge when a therapist tries to influence the process of separation by allowing private customs to intrude on the behavior of clients when parting company. It has already been noted that termination with some families should occur while traces of tension or unsolved problems remain.

From the perspective of treating a family it is easy for the therapist to succumb, rather innocently, to an expectation that pushes for a display of warmth and affection among family members before terminating treatment. There are, however, relationships in which warmth and affection are rarely, if ever, experienced, and if encouraged to act this role would transgress a preferred distance. A progression of feelings, states, stages, if you will, are commonly associated with separation, and it is to this that a note of caution is raised: to assume that everyone will experience a series of progressive "warming" stages in order to successfully complete a separation is a questionable requirement.

Admittedly, a show of tenderness between a couple who otherwise practice disaffection is a welcome sign that suggests therapy has, indeed, changed the relationship, but this can no more be a goal than opting to teach people how to be spontaneous. Affection, if it is to come, is a by-product of an experience and to this extent cannot become a primary objective at termination, lest it seem staged or mechanistic.

Relationships can be quite satisfactory, rewarding, or productive without obvious signs of affection, and the ability to terminate therapy with a family when less-than-love is in evidence is essential.

4. Summary

This work evolved from changes in the field of family therapy within the context of related changes in the social order. With respect to the former, family conflict was conceived to be a response to maladaptive communication patterns among family members, and symptomatology a result of this prolonged conflict. Intrapsychic paradigms common to explanations of psychopathology were replaced by communication models of behavior. From this new perspective, symptoms were redefined "as a way of dealing with another person." (Haley, 1963, p. 4.) This redefinition meant that a symptom was no longer understood as a defense against an idea, or an unconscious thought threatening to become conscious, but rather it was a way of handling or disarming another person in a relationship. This moved symptoms into communication processes. Haley (1963) explains that for a symptom to evolve, "the patient's behavior must be extreme in its influence on someone else and he must indicate in some way that he cannot help behaving as he does." (p. 5.) Concurrently, changes in the social order and the emerging women's movement reciprocally influenced one another as traditional sex role stereotypes were brought under question. Both series of events, the first in family therapy, the second in male-female relationships, required additional changes in the treatment of the family unit. Emphasis upon communication models in therapy encouraged the growth of a number of treatment strategies designed to alter and restructure the observable behaviors of family members toward one another. Haley (1963) writes:

It will be argued here that a patient's symptoms are perpetuated by the way he himself behaves and by the influence of other people intimately involved with him. It follows that psychotherapeutic tactics should be designed to persuade the individual to change his behavior and/or persuade his intimates to change their behavior in relation to him. (p. 6)

Similarly, changing role definitions of men and women required a renewed perspective upon restructuring not only maladaptive behavior patterns, but also social definitions circumscribing role functions by virtue of gender. Naturally, not every family therapist who shifted his/

her theoretical framework from an intrapsychic to a communication model of behavior responded to both therapeutic and social change. It was still possible to gear treatment goals toward achieving a more harmonious and socially adaptive family unit along conventional sex role lines. On the other hand, therapists who were influenced by social change were faced with a particular theoretical problem. Conceiving that social forms were important factors in the production of family stress and individual symptomatology, the requirement to develop a theoretical model which would account for and respond to this influence became apparent. Spiegel (1971) developed a theoretical model which conceptualized dynamic relationships between systems larger than the individual and the family. He describes this model as follows:

Structurally, most small groups are described as fitting into a network which constitutes an extended system or organization. Nuclear family groups belong to extended chains of relatives; baseball teams belong to leagues; work groups are part of industrial, commercial, or service organizations. All such organizations and extended systems are themselves fitted into even more extensively structural systems—the family system, the occupational system, the political system, etc.—of the overall society. Functionally, small groups are described as performing services for the maintenance of the larger systems to which they belong; in turn, these more extended systems perform essential services for their small groups in a reciprocal process. (p. 51)

While this model enlarged the understanding of human affairs with respect to the interrelationship of systems, it did not directly change the treatment modality of family therapy. Strategies for therapeutic change continued to be circumscribed around the unit most workable in this regard—the family system itself. Haley (1976) speaks to this: "Whatever radical position he [the therapist] takes as a citizen, his obligation as a therapist is to define the social unit that he can change to solve the presenting problem of a client." (p. 5.) Similarly, Minuchin (1974) writes, "the target of intervention in the present is the family system." (p. 14.) Both Haley and Minuchin recognized larger socio-cultural forces as influential in shaping intrafamilial behavior, yet neither of them envisions a way to respond to suprasystem forces in treatment. As a result, therapy, despite its changes in the theory of psychopathology, continued to focus upon improving intrafamilial relations by realigning the family to work within the larger social order. Conversely, a growing number of family therapists have taken social change seriously in their treatment methods. Rice and Rice (1977) developed a treatment model encouraging therapists to become more sensitive to conflict in couples who were influenced by changing "marital" life styles and values. Techniques toward this end include: "a) working out a schedule for sharing household and child care responsibilities; b) elaborating and revising the marital 'contract'; c) trying out separation experiences; d) exploring open companionship." From their position, Rice and Rice state: "We feel this type of therapy can free men and women from sex role stereotyped patterns of relatedness and help them to form interpersonal bonds that offer possibilities for enhanced personal and conjoint growth." (p. 9.) It is this form of family therapy that lies closest to the writer's theoretical model for change.

What has been missing is a theory which lays the groundwork for conserving the family system while liberating individual family members. It is the writer's thesis that enlarging upon interchanging male/ female roles does not *a priori* build a case for liberation. Liberation is possible when an individual, or a group of individuals (family) are not conditionally governed by currents of social change—whenever or whatever direction this change assumes. On the contrary, if liberated, they are as likely to resist change as they are to welcome it. Liberation, from the writer's standpoint, means that people are able to analyze, reject, or accept long-standing or newly developing social norms as they see fit; they are not made increasingly more flexible in their abilities to adjust, but instead are made critically aware of the social and psychological implications of their respective roles in the social scheme. In short, "liberated" individuals can choose from a range of options without prematurely constricting their choices.

Consciousness-raising, reviewed and discussed in the writings of Chesler (1970), Gornick (1971), Mander and Rush (1974) and Steiner (1971) develop a theoretical model in which liberation of an individual requires an analysis of problems, both from a personal and political context. As a model for change, insight from an intrapsychic perspective is supplemented, and in many cases replaced by awareness; an experience through which an individual comes to understand his or her behavior as a function of socio-political forms and not deep intrapsychic conflict. Problem solving from this vantage point is markedly different from what occurs in more conventional forms of psychodynamically oriented treatment. There is often as much emphasis placed upon changing one's circumstances as there is upon changing oneself.

Any effort to change one's circumstances may not necessarily diminish anxiety; however, it may release the frustration which builds in people when they experience themselves as helpless victims of social force and change. However, there is a problem. Feminist writers, who have strongly favored consciousness-raising for women in order that they might free themselves from traditional institutional forms, have issued declarations in which the baby was being thrown out with the bathwater. Decrying all social institutions as male dominated, liberation demanded the overthrow of the nuclear family; it was understood that the nuclear family is an inherent bulwark for the capitalistic-male-dominated system. Naturally, traditional therapy and family therapy in particular cannot be anything but handmaidens of the state. Conceiving liberation through family therapy would stand as an indefensible argument; any institution dedicated to the maintenance of the family unit stands in opposition to liberation. Ferocious in their attack upon the family, many feminists were blinded to anything positive which the family might promote. Arguments often blurred the distinction between hierarchy as a function of age and experience, and patriarchy as a function of socio-cultural myth. It was a short step from there to the furtherance of ideas denouncing all male-female relationships as bastions of oppression. Although many feminists refuted any distinctions short of anatomical ones which differentiated men from women, the force of their arguments paradoxically sounded as though it were the biological differences *per se* that they were desperately fighting to overcome.

Regardless of the composition, size, or the politics of a human group, infants and children are dependent upon adults for survival. Age is a function of this relationship and a hierarchal order is the rule, at least until a child gains a degree of self-sufficiency. Demanding basic needs by the child can be oppressive to either parent. The lifting of oppression in a parent-child relationship herein requires a sustained effort, not to liberate oneself as a parent, but to liberate one's child from requiring continuous parenting. If the nuclear family were made obsolete, the problem with oppression and hierarchical authority would still be inherent in a mother-child bond. Recommendations were made for a variety of communal settings where cybernetic socialism would completely replace traditional family forms (Firestone, 1970). This, however, still does not solve the more fundamental problem of age difference and dependency of infant upon mother. Barber (1976), examining a number of different collectives, reported that many familiar power struggles peculiar to conventional families erupted within communal organizations. If liberation for women requires total independence from men, then what will happen to the male child, born to a liberated woman, and dependent upon her for survival? The issue is not how to annihilate the nuclear family unit, but how to transform it and still enhance individual growth and development.

The family in therapy seemed to offer a workable unit in which liberation of individuals and the conservation of a system may be simultaneously conceivable. Whether healthy or sick, there is a commitment built into it which is already present at the onset of treatment. While the war rages, it is more a war of politics than of gender. Many diehard feminists reached for explanations in social history to explain the struggles of women for power. Unfortunately, they were often so blinded with rage they refused to see any positive elements in the nuclear family form. Hobbs (1970) speaks to this and points out how marriage can serve as a potential assurance against many privations of later years of life. Yet she takes umbrage against the notion that commitment automatically means a traditional marriage. Underscoring the growing need to be loved and to love, particularly in one's middle years, Hobbs speaks of liberation as a function of many new freedoms. "There is no reason, for instance," writes Hobbs (1970),

why skilled women cannot work and support the family if the husband would prefer to stay home, do the housework and look after the children. There is no reason why man and wife cannot both work half-time and share equally the care of the house and children. There is no law that states that all married couples must spend every day and night of their lives together. . . . The institution of marriage in the future can be justified only if it assumes a totally new form and totally new freedoms. (p. 144)

It is to this idea that the writer has attempted to combine the practice of family therapy with the process of consciousness-raising. At best, what has been presented in this book stands as a first effort. The potential for development and variations on this model for change is limitless. It is hoped that not only will consciousness-raising liberate people as it strengthens a family unit, but eventually, in some significant way, it will also effect change in larger social institutions as well. If it is true that the family is a cornerstone of the social system, a transformation of family structure on a large enough scale will transform the institutions supported by it. While this represents an optimistic view, social change is already shaking many of the traditional structures of the larger social system.

Perhaps family therapy can help family members resonate to social change and have a decided hand in shaping its direction. In this manner, only inflexible and repressive forms need disintegrate, and not the family unit itself.

Limitations on a Theory and its Application

The development of a theoretical model for change proposes to combine two divergent processes: consciousness-raising as liberating, and family therapy as conservative. What are some of the anticipated difficulties inherent in such a juxtaposition? And what are some of the limitations? A note of caution is essential. The concept of liberation must not be overextended or mythologized. One mode of evaluating a case for liberation would require attention to its opposite. This is particularly true if the endeavor of a therapeutic model is toward the conservation of the family unit. While consciousness-raising may be successful in detaching a family from automatically believing myths spawned through the social system, it is just as possible to sell the idea of "freedom" as representing a complete independence from social institutions and their constraints—another myth, to be sure. What can result is a change from despair and hopelessness to rage and frenzied acting out.

The acceptance of constraints as often temporary and at times necessary is essential for the survival of the family unit. Structure provides support and the frequency with which behavior is repeated and ritualized enables family members to achieve a sense of nurturance. The notion of constraints allows one to consider alternative choices, using the very constraint as a foil for its opposite.

A second anticipated problem can result from overattending to social issues. Linking family problems to broad social issues can lead to an overwhelming sense of frustration. For example, a case can be made where family problems are systematically traced, not just to surrounding social institutions, but to areas so large as to embrace the entire planet. Therapeutically, this would create a contract for lifelong treatment. Instead of clarifying and focusing, the family would become immobilized, since change in any one direction would require change in another. To avoid such a mishap, a clear understanding of the limitations of consciousness-raising is necessary. Sharpening awareness means that consciousness-raising may have to confine its focus. At best, it can provide for a skillful analysis of selecting out of the social world order those issues which have a direct bearing upon the family in treatment.

While the limitations of consciousness-raising are respected, attention to the sex of the therapist involved in a consciousness-raising endeavor may make a decided difference in the process. Debra Cohen, summarizing recent research in the newsline of *Psychology Today* (May 1977, p. 92) reports that the sex of the therapist produces differing effects upon women patients, depending upon their age, marital status, etc. As an example, young single women were more concerned with "active responses" from a male therapist. They were more inhibited, less open and self-possessed, hence they required active approval and encouragement from the therapist. With a female therapist, women between the ages of 23 and 28 felt themselves less critical and believed they were receiving more encouragement. Finally, researchers reported that those women affected by the sex of their therapist were also those who were judged to be under the greatest societal pressure to conform to socially acceptable lifestyles and social norms. A male therapist involved in the practice of family therapy presents to many individuals the symbol of the male patriarch empowered to heal the family and set it upon its rightful course. If a male therapist gives permission or emphasis to liberation a problem emerged. To what extent can a woman in the family autonomously choose a "liberated" course so long as a man is in charge? A similar problem arises when the therapist is a female: can the "maternal" figure be seen as generating choices for family members? The extent to which the sex of the therapist has an impact on the system is an area requiring attention and exploration.

It is necessary to consider the limitations of the model itself. Fundamental to this is the realization that unknown and unanticipated factors beset the field of human affairs more profoundly than any other applied science. While we are dealing with systems, and may believe we have taken a thorough accounting of the systems impinging upon a family, there must be an overriding assumption that unknown parameters may produce markedly unanticipated outcomes. Respecting the concept of paradox, it may be possible to work toward liberation and achieve an opposite result: that the family chooses to live by a more highly structured model of hierarchy than was true before.

Ultimately, the choice of lifestyle must lie with the family itself. The very best this model can hope for is a resolution of the conflict presented in therapy and an enlargement of the family's options to live free of some of the social myths that have constricted individual and collective development.

NOTES

Chapter 1

1. Burgess (1960) traces the development of the nuclear family. He cites the rural colonial family as the first functional social group and work collective. The farm had a manager (father), a foreman (mother) and workers of various degrees of skill (relatives and children). In an environment of semi-isolation, the family had to depend upon its members for most of its needs. (p. 58.)

An extensive history of the nuclear family in Colonial times is researched by Goodsell (1926). In that period, families had many children due to the high mortality rates. Family discipline and religious training was very strict as the church assumed a major socializing function for isolated families. As industrialization increased, the fracturing of the family into units, each going about their business in separate ways, took hold. Compulsory education laws took care of the children, as they were now clearly segregated into a distinct grouping, with predetermined tasks to accomplish. They no longer were of primary importance in helping the family to survive. (pp. 341-411.)

2. Howells (1971) defines the nuclear family, sometimes labeled an "immediate family," or an "elementary family" as "a sub-system of the social system, consisting of two adults of different sexes who undertake a parenting role to one or more children." (p. 9.) Murdock (1949) states that of 192 societies studied, 47 (24%) have a nuclear unit as the basic family form. (p. 41.)

While the nuclear family unit is considered a small social system, Tec (1975) offers statistics indicating that it is still diminishing in size. According to recent census figures, in 1974 the average household included fewer than three people, compared to 1960, with an average of 3.3, and 1950, at an average of 3.39 (N.Y. Times, 1975). He further concludes that in "Contemporary America," the small and related household is not only the most frequently encountered type, but is also the one which enjoys the fullest normative support. (p. 228.)

3. The biological family is examined in Firestone (1970). She lists four fundamental, "if not immutable facts" which influenced a belief that sex differences underscore the development of a class system based upon sex.

[1] Women at the continual mercy of their biology—menstruation, menopause, painful childbirth, etc.—before the advent of birth control.

[2] The length of time it takes human infants to grow to independence.

[3] Mother/child dependency in every human society.

[4] Natural reproductive differences between the sexes led to divisions of labor at the origin of class and caste. (pp. 8-9.)

4. Foci, according to Spiegel (1971) refers to areas in the transactional field such as: Universe, Culture, Society, Group, Psyche, Soma, each of which is a

system composed of essentially the same processes. Together they comprise the total transactional field.

For example, a nuclear family may be embroiled in controversy, with a school—say, over the propriety of a child praying or not praying in school—while, at the same time, it receives support from the extended family system to which it is connected. The support indicates the equivalence of norms controlling the role of the student between the family and its supporters. In this model, the family is considered the group; the school is the society; the student is the psyche. Tension between each foci is the method through which Spiegel conceptualizes transactional processes. (p. 52.)

5. The relationship of the nuclear family and the larger social order is defined by Deckard (1975). She writes:

The nuclear family, in which the husband is the major breadwinner, also serves the important functions in a capitalist society. As an economic unit, the nuclear family is a valuable stabilizing force in capitalistic society. Because the husband is solely responsible for supporting his wife and children, his ability to strike or to change jobs is limited. Because his wife is economically dependent, she is also likely to become emotionally dependent and passive. Thus, her economic vulnerability is apt to make her fearful and interested only in security. Therefore, she will exert a conservative influence on her husband and children. The family, as currently organized, keeps both men and women from making trouble. (p. 416.)

Howells (1971) describes the family as a subsystem of the social order. (p. 9.) The primary functions of the family are listed, one of which is to form an economic unit. (p. 11.)

Goodman, David (1972), cites the fundamental purposes of the family as an American social subsystem. Some of his prescriptions are: work as the great healer; persistence; objectivity; and a democratic household. In our troubled times, Goodman pleads for stronger patriotism to combat the powerful foreign enemies out to destroy us. This article was featured in a major reference work in marital and family therapy. (pp. 318-331.)

Minuchin (1974) describes the family as an interface between the individual and the social order. He concludes that the "family functions serve two different ends. One is internal—the psychosocial protection of its members; the other is external—the accommodation to a culture and the transmission of that culture." (p. 46.)

6. Firestone (1970) traces the history of the developing myth of childhood, determining that it was at the end of the sixteenth century when the concept of childhood actually took hold. (pp. 76-91.) While childhood as a separate entity did not exist before this period of history, it is possible that the high mortality rates might also have made the concept of childhood unnecessary. Since a person's life span at this period of history was markedly shorter, when science improved health care for families, this may have also been a factor in

developing the notion of childhood. If people ordinarily did not live much beyond their thirties, it would seem absurd to keep them in a prolonged state of childhood dependency.

7. Harland (1902) edited a handbook for women. In it she points out one of the responsibilities of a mother. "It is not much to say, that when the mother teaches her baby girl to lie quiet in the cradle, she is giving her her first lesson as a homemaker. For the prime quality of the homemaker should be self-control, and this is her earliest instruction to that great study. . . . Obedience is the cornerstone of self-control, and the child cannot learn it too soon." (p. vii)

With respect to women and formal education, Harland writes:

> In our public schools there is a wise effort in progress to give the girls of the higher grades some practical familiarity with cooking and cognate subjects. I do not think there is any movement of the kind on foot in any college for women. . . . Is it unreasonable to ask that there should be furnished to women the chance to take, as an elective or as a final study, a course in that science to which most of them will devote their future lives? (p. xiv)

Lest the reader believe this text to be one of many, it is important to be familiar with some of its contributors. This will shed some light upon the power evoked in the ideas quoted above. Articles have been included from such distinguished figures as: Hon. Theodore Roosevelt, former President of the U.S.; Hon. Grover Cleveland, former President of the U.S.; Hon. George F. Hoar, Senator from Massachusetts; Hon. Seth Low, Mayor of New York, etc.

8. According to research published in *Women's Rights Almanac* (1974), the following statistics were amassed by Arlene Alligood. In 1973, 1) Women made up only 3% of the entire U.S. Congress. 2) No women sat in the U.S. Senate and only 16 in the House of Representatives—3.7%. 3) Of 33 Senate races in 1972, only 6 involved women, all of whom were defeated. 4) Women made up less than 6% of State legislators—424 women among 7,700 members. 5) No women were governors or lieutenant governors. 6) Only 4.3% of the mayors in the 1,000 largest cities were women; and only 3.6% of the mayors in the 750 cities of over 30,000 population were women. 7) The results were not appreciably better within the Federal labor force. In jobs at the top of the scale—where the pay starts at $30,000—there were 191 women and 10,268 men. (p. 541.)

Investigation of poverty and welfare, researched by Sallie E. Williams, concluded: 1) Women are more likely to be unemployed than men. In 1972, the rate of unemployment for women over 20 years was 5.5 compared to 3.9 for men. 2) Women were generally in low-paying, dead-end jobs, such as clerical, service, and household employment. 3) In 1971, women as heads of families with median incomes of $5,115 compared to men receiving $10,930. (pp. 545-549.)

While these figures suggest some change in the large institutions and commercial marketplace with respect to women, they continue to reflect the differences between male/female political and economic power.

9. While Axelson's (1963) study was interesting, it was conducted in a small western town where conventional attitudes toward women working may have been strongly negative, even if economics were not the primary issue. The study did suggest that the changing social role for women is slower in translating itself back into the family.

10. The latest census on women in the job market was taken in 1975 and published in *Newsday* (1977). The data indicate: The total female labor force was 45.9% of the female population in 1975. Weekly earnings of full-time female employees between the ages of 16 and 24 was $117 per week; males in the same age-range group earned $149. Women who were 25 years and over earned a median salary of $146, while males in the same age range earned $235. (p. 184.)

Ferree's (1976) work indicates that many women were quite dissatisfied with the characteristics of their work in the job market. Although they were happier than when staying home with the household chores, they indicated that their husbands' work, even when they were employed, was more interesting than their own. Many wished that their daughters would grow up to be different from themselves. (p. 76.)

A study conducted in *Long Island,* a weekend *Newsday* magazine (Feb 20, 1977) shed some interesting light on the outcome upon women who are consistently in a lower-salaried position than men. Sampling 482 working people, it was determined that the kind of job a person holds has some effect upon his or her attitude toward a hypothetical situation—"Would you still work if you won the million dollar lottery?" The results were that the higher the income, the more likely the worker was to state that he or she would continue working. Of those earning above $25,000, 77% would continue working, while 56% of those earning between $10,000 and $15,000 would continue employment. Since women and other minority groups are consistently lower in salaries than men, the effect upon their personal sense of competence and achievement is evident.

11. Divorce was also studied by Tec (1975). He concluded that the isolated nuclear unit places inordinate demands upon its members for affection, companionship and all other gratifications. The strain leading to divorce can be traced directly to the enormous burden of meeting these mutual expectations. "To a large extent," writes Tec, "such unfulfilled expectations become a major reason for our high divorce rates. This in turn suggests that marriages do not break up because they are taken lightly, rather, they break up because too much is expected of them."

Despite this, statistics published in the *Woman's Almanac* (1974) reflect a steady commitment to marriage. The divorce rate, although climbing steadily through 1960-1972, has remained constantly lower than the rate of marriage. (p. 479.)

12. All data have been taken from *State of the Child New York City* (Lash & Sigal, 1976).

Out-of-Wedlock Births: In 1974 60% were black, 20% white, and 20% Puerto Rican. Slightly more than 47% of all back babies born in New York City in 1974 were born out of wedlock. While it is in dispute whether being born out of wedlock and growing up in a fatherless family is detrimental *per se* to the health of a child, the existing evidence does prove that these children are likely to be born into poverty and this association alone makes illegitimate birth a risk factor for a child. (p. 25.)

Abortions: Of the abortions performed in 1974, 48.6% were for black women, 37.4% were for white women, and 14% were for Puerto Ricans. There were 4,800 more abortions than live births to black women in 1974. Many abortions represent a failure to use methods of birth control or ineffective contraceptive practice. The Alan Guttmacher Institute has estimated that there are some 106,200 women of low and marginal income who are in need of family planning services, but who are not served by organized programs or private physicians. (pp. 25-26.)

13. Lash and Sigal (1976) offer the following statistics on children's health and mortality:

[1] Infant mortality rates and low birth-weight ratios are higher for black and Puerto Rican babies than for white babies, and higher for New York City than for the nation as a whole.

[2] Children born out of wedlock and those born to drug-addicted mothers evidence much higher rates of infant mortality and low birth-weight.

[3] Over the past decade, homicide has accounted for an increasing proportion of child death.

[4] Hospitals, as opposed to private physicians, are the primary source of care for children from low-income families. (p. 44.)

Minuchin (1974) refers to studies in psychosomatic medicine citing findings that the child responds to stresses affecting the family through psychophysical changes in blood chemistry. Diabetes and other conditions such as allergies, etc., have a significant relationship to changes in family stress. (pp. 7-9.)

14. Lash and Sigal (1976) offer the following statistics on education.

A child in New York City with respect to education faces the following situation:

[1] As of April, 1974, two-thirds of the public school children in New York City were not able to read at their grade level.

[2] Large numbers of children are absent from school. The official record indicates for 1973-74, approximately 195,000 public school students, or 17.7% of enrollment, were out of school each day.

[3] Student suspensions from public schools have increased by 66.7% since 1969-70. High school suspensions increased by 249.7%.

[4] There were 6,817 reported evidence of crime and violence in the city's schools in 1974-75. 63.6% more than in the previous year.

[5]In 1973-74, over 34,000 New York City students dropped out of high school. (p. 58.)

In a study of over 300 schools in a New York state survey, Bronfenbrenner (1973) reports that 58% of the variation in student achievement was predicted by three socioeconomic factors—broken homes, overcrowded housing, and education of the head of the household. (p. 156.)

15. A study (Lash & Sigal, 1976) analyzing the reasons given for the placement of children speaks to the increasing pain of family crisis and conflict. Foster-care placement usually occurs because of parental problems rather than child problems. Prominent among these are parental inability to cope (cited in 27.7% of the cases), neglect of child (14.1%), abandonment of child (11.6%), and mental illness of parent (11.6%).

Examining the above, all but 20% of the 29,000 city children in foster care in 1974 were black and Puerto Rican. More than half of them were children of female-headed families on public assistance; more than half were born out of wedlock. (pp. 61-66.)

16. Child abuse is covered in the work of Lash and Sigal (1975). With respect to data on child abuse, during 1973, there were 3,086 alleged abuse cases reported to the Central Registry in New York City. Once again, nonwhite families had a consistently higher rate of child abuse from 1969 to 1974. This is consistent with all other figures from a socioeconomic perspective. (pp. 77-80.)

Testimony given by Bronfenbrenner (1973) reported that the most severe injuries on children were inflicted by the mother in single-parent households . . . a statistic which Bronfenbrenner believes reflective of the desperation faced by young mothers today. (p. 153.)

17. Howell's (1971) article, entitled "The Psychopathogenesis of Hard-Core Families" is published in his larger text, *Theory and Practice of Family Psychiatry* (1971, pp. 459-468). This study is a remarkable view on the relationship between family stress and socioeconomic structure. The author examines a family's behavior in the most abject squalor and draws the conclusion that it is their emotional instability which causes the squalor. What happens to an individual growing up under such conditions is ignored, as if anyone, despite his circumstances, can rise up and achieve. If Howell's reasoning were accepted, it would mean that slums are caused by the intrapsychic disturbance of their inhabitants. Testimony by Bronfenbrenner (1973) to the Senate Committee on Public Welfare, as well as the sweeping research study completed by Lash and Sigal (1971) offers voluminous data contrary to the work of Howell. In almost every instance, social conditions have been intimately tied into causing severe family dysfunction and individual psychopathology.

18. Koch and Koch (1976) make a strong pitch for marital enrichment programs for those couples who desire increased intimacy and satisfaction. Distinguishing marriage enrichment from marriage counseling, the former is identified as dealing with relationships in which the couple believe their

marriage to be good but decide that there is room for improvement and growth. (pp. 33-34, 83, 95, 95.)

Chapter 2

1. Nathan Ackerman was one of the earliest pioneers in family therapy beginning in the late 1940s. In 1957 he founded the first family treatment mental health clinic in New York City.

In 1954, Murray Bowen began treating families at the National Institute for Mental Health. At a similar time, Lyman Wynne worked with families through the NIMH while Boszormenji-Nagy (1965) organized the Family Therapy Project at the Eastern Pennsylvania Psychiatric Institute—a psychoanalytic approach to family treatment.

In 1958, Don Jackson began family studies at the Mental Research Institute in Palo Alto, California. There the focus was on the study of schizophrenia. The project director was Gregory Bateson (1952-1962). His influence had much to do with introducing a systems approach to investigating communication patterns, rather than intrapsychic elements. A comprehensive history of the development of marital and family therapy is published in *A Decade of Family Research and Action:* National Council on Family Relations (1970, pp. 3-24, 241-278).

2. There is opinion suggesting that family therapy developed by a group of maverick psychiatrists disenchanted with traditional modes of treatment. Observations were made that when patients were treated and returned home, symptoms of a dysfunctional marriage followed. According to Olson (1970) the significant breakthrough occurred as a result of a misunderstanding by John Bell. Reportedly he had read John Bowlby's account of experience with families "and misinterpreted the report to mean treatment of the family unit." After John Bell's report, others then began to speak more openly about their experiences with families in treatment. (p. 244.)

3. An interesting conclusion of Fleck's studies was that one of the characteristic forms of family dysfunction related to schizophrenia was a handicapping of a child in achieving sexual identity and maturity by the parents' uncertainty over their own sex roles.

4. Haley (1963) takes a classical psychoanalytic symptom of compulsive handwashing and explains it through communication theory. He describes a woman's symptoms as a desperate way of dealing with her husband, and also as a method of protecting him from facing his own problems and the other difficulties in their marriage. (p. 15.)

5. A comprehensive review of the work of Jackson, Satir, Haley, Bateson, Weakland and Riskin is published in an article by Joel Fischer (1974) in which he reviews the work evolving from the mental Research Institute in Palo Alto, California. The theoretical perspectives on family pathology are divided into four major approaches to family therapy: (a) Communication theory; (b) role

theory; (c) intrapsychically-oriented ego theory; and (d) game or strategy theory (definition of networks of relationships in which people place themselves and definition of reciprocating behavior in those networks). (pp. 105-140.)

6. Watzlawick, Weakland, and Fisch (1974) developed brief therapy based upon theories of groups and the theory of logical types. Their work was greatly influenced by the writings of Gregory Bateson and Ashby's model of the homeostasis. (p. 16.)

The concept of homeostasis received considerable attention as a model in which to understand family process and change. This work was developed out of Palo Alto by Jackson (1965).

7. Spiegel (1971) moved away from Whitehead's conception of process and of the world as an organism, so that the study of human behavior could be circumscribed and understood in its own light. Spiegel's objective was to construct a model to observe and describe intersystemic relations. He developed a model of a transactional field, where each region was a "foci," meaning that each area represented a region of knowledge about systems of similar processes with the total field. The following is his model. (p. 42.)

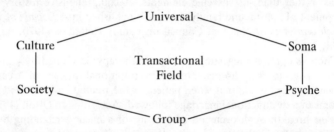

8. Spiegel's understanding of social role is defined as "a goal-directed configuration of acts patterned in accordance with cultural value orientations for the position a person holds in a social group or situation." While he acknowledged that "the role of a parent is to bring up children," or that "the role of an educator is to educate," various cultures interpret the role behavior differently. (p. 189.)

9. In his text, Spiegel (1971) presents a comprehensive picture of a second-generation Italian-American Roman Catholic family. In this case, the struggle of the Tondis family with the neighborhood and wider community is examined in light of the pressures of acculturation upon them. (pp. 201-264.)

10. A comprehensive review of 26 techniques of family and marital therapy is outlined by Friedman (1947).

Despite the obvious departure of many techniques from traditional models of therapy, they are radical, only in the discipline of family therapy itself. They are *conservative* in that all of them are used to reconstruct the family as a workable, harmonious subsystem in the social order. (pp. 259-263.)

A comprehensive review of marital and family therapy has been published by

Olson (1970). A census of the American Association of Marital Counselors (1968) broke down professional affiliations as follows: 19%—psychology; 19%—social work; 14%—ministry; 8%—sociology; 26%—marital therapist. Seventy-five percent belong to a second discipline rooted in traditional training and theory. With respect to family therapists, a recent survey conducted by the Group for the Advancement of Psychiatry found that 40% of the therapists were social workers and another 40% were psychiatrists and psychologists.

According to the research, the pioneers in family therapy were heavily weighted in psychiatry. As a result, psychodynamic conceptualizations of behavior were highly favored as theoretical models. (pp. 241-278.)

11. Minuchin (1974) understands the therapist's role to be that in which families are helped to restructure themselves in order that they can become more efficient social units. He writes, "the family is a social unit that faces a series of developmental tasks." Such tasks include: establishing routines in early marriage; separating from each family of origin; an organization of work, duties, pleasures, etc.; care and nurturance of a newborn infant; "children become adolescents and then adults. New siblings join the family, or the parents become grandparents." A "normal family," as it is called, moves and changes according to these tasks. "Change," he writes, "always moves from society to the family, never from the smaller unit to the larger." Thus, Minuchin gears his model of change in this predetermined direction. (pp. 16-52.)

Bell (1962) writes, "family group therapy is, then, a treatment method which depends on the presence and control of the therapist. He uses his own personal and social skills to help a family attain what it has shown itself unable to reach before, the ability to live for its own welfare, for the welfare of each of its family members, and ultimately for the betterment of the community."

12. Howells (1966) lists social problems attributed to individual psychopathology: alcoholism, illegitimacy, delinquency, criminality, divorce, suicide, child neglect, and unhappiness despite material wealth. In his conclusion, Howells considers "Vector therapy" as one of the psychiatric solutions. This entails the psychiatrist arranging community services to troubled families. The political power they are granted is to decide issues such as separating children from unhealthy and depriving mothers, etc. (p. 1,159.)

Contrary to such a position, Bronfenbrenner (1973) has researched factors contributing to family disorganization and the development of psychopathology. Of primary importance, Bronfenbrenner attributes these outcomes to the following: "That the forces of disorganization arise primarily not from within the family itself, but from the circumstances in which the family finds itself and the way of life which these circumstances, in turn, impose" (p. 155). "The first symptoms," writes the author, "occur in the emotional and motivational sphere and are manifested in disaffection, indifference, irresponsibility, and an inability to follow through in activities requiring application and persistence." (p. 156.)

13. It seems as if Haley's (1976) recognition of the social influence upon families is met with a sense of frustration; while he realizes that he is in the business to put families together, they are apt to be torn apart once again by the social institutions.

14. An interesting research study by Scott (1974) examined the manner in which the label "well" or "ill" is given to an individual in a family. He found that what families considered as "well" was directly associated with the values that were specific to particular families. The assumption that patients enter a mental hospital because they are "ill" was questioned. The research suggested that illness had much to do with behavior that was untenable in a patient's community situation. It was concluded that while mental illness is not a myth, entering a hospital because of illness is a myth. Patients desiring help can find it outside a hospital setting. Thus, an admission may not be a mentally ill person, yet all who are admitted are assumed to be mentally ill—a finding in harmony with Szasz's writings. It was also determined that a family decided who was ill before a doctor arrived, and often the patient, calling the doctor immediately got the label "ill." (pp. 58-73.)

15. Szasz's (1960, 1970) work has consistently indicted the mental health field for disguising politics under the rug of therapy.

16. The history of the women's movement is published in: Altbach, 1974; Gager, 1974; Deckard, 1975; *Women's Role in Contemporary Society*, 1972; Firestone, 1970; Janeway, 1972.

17. Chesler's (1971) main thesis is that conventional psychotherapy is extremely destructive to women. Her assertions are that most therapists hold rigid stereotypical beliefs about women, their inferiority, etc. Psychology has not only failed to help women change, but has actually oppressed women who have attempted to break conventional sex role behavior.

Weisstein (1971) asserts that "psychology has nothing to say about what women are really like, what they need and what they want, essentially because psychology does not really know." (p. 135.)

A study on women by Broverman, Broverman, Clarkson, Rosenkranz, and Vogel (1970) concludes that mental health practitioners tend to perceive healthy women somewhat less healthy than healthy men. The results of their study revealed that clinicians (a) held different mental health standards for males and females; (b) held standards for the two sexes which conformed to stereotypes of mental health for males and for adults, sex unspecified, but held different standards for females.

Pietrofesa and Schlossberg (1970) studied counselor bias against women entering masculine occupations. They discovered that there was a definite bias in male and female counselors against women planning to enter such fields as engineering, etc.

Bernard (1971) found clinicians tend to encourage women to accept themselves as less important than men. In this way, a marriage would have a greater opportunity to succeed.

Research by Thomas and Stewart (1971) determined that high school counselors (18 female, 44 male) showed the trends: (a) female counselors gave higher acceptance scores concerning women who chose male oriented occupations (engineering) than did male counselors; (b) all counselors rated those clients who selected more stereotypical occupational choices (women to home economics) as people who tend to make a more appropriate career choice ($p <$ .05). It was determined that female clients who chose deviate career goals were judged to be more in need of counseling, yet would find counseling more of a hindrance than a help to them.

18. Firestone (1970) does cite certain biological factors influential in the development of patriarchy. She cites: (a) women at mercy of female biology—pregnancy, menstruation, etc.; (b) human infants' prolonged dependency; (c) interdependency between mother and child in every culture; (d) reproductive difference between sexes established first divisions of labor. Her point is that despite these givens, the sexual imbalance of power is unjustified. "Thus," writes Firestone, "the natural is not necessarily a 'human' value." (pp. 9-10.)

19. The history and myths of childhood are discussed in Firestone (1970) and Farson (1974).

20. Firestone (1970) reveals how modern school education and other institutions were articulations of new concepts of childhood. Children were effectively segregated further from the adult world for longer periods of time. (pp. 181-183.)

Philip Aries (1975) discusses the problems this developing concept produced. Speaking of affection and love, Aries comments that before childhood and the separation of the nuclear family was complete, sentiment was a by-product of families. Now it too becomes a requirement. The contemporary family as we know it was born when society began setting children apart from adults. This transformation gave socializing and educating functions to institutions, and thus, affection became the primary function of the family. With this as a goal, it is understandable to consider the possible failure in this, and the pain as a result. (pp. 53-58.)

Bronfenbrenner (1973) offers testimony to the U.S. Senate regarding the disastrous consequences which result from the segmentation of families and the isolation of children. He states, "By isolating our children from the rest of society, we abandon them to a world devoid of adults and ruled by the destructive impulses and compelling pressures both of the age-segregated peer group and the aggressive and exploitative television screen, we leave our children bereft of standards and support and our own lives impoverished and corrupt." (p. 434.)

21. Farson (1974) discussed the problems resulting from compulsory schooling. (pp. 96-112.) He points out the social ramifications if compulsory education were abolished. "Without doubt, ending compulsory education will change a great many institutions other than education itself. It raises the prospect of children working, entering the labor force at an early age. It changes our idea

of home and family, of child care and parental responsibility. Again, it is impossible to change one element of the system without experiencing widespread system change." (p. 99.)

22. Gornick (1971) provides case presentations of women's consciousness-raising experience in order that one may view the process as it unfolds.

23. The fact that men are rarely in a situation where they talk about personal feelings and emotions from a perspective of examining their need for power makes the observation cited by Farrell understandable. It is only as a patient in psychotherapy, where men will place themselves in the hands of an authority figure, that they will divulge the intimacies of their lives. In consciousness-raising groups men are asking for personal help from their peers as they put themselves on the line without the trappings of masculine power. As Farrell (1974) points out, the men come to understand that their main weakness is harboring the expectation of not being weak. (p. 222.)

Transcripts of men's consciousness-raising groups are provided in Farrell (1974, pp. 234-321).

24. Nichol's (1975) discusses the relationship between male consciousness and the socioeconomic system. He explains that the social chaos of today is only a symptom of more fundamental problems rooted in the values to which men subscribe. He writes, "and since men control most businesses, these values were reflected through the economic and technological structures they create. Today's machine economy is only an echo of traditional male attitudes. It is these attitudes that must change before a dent can be made in the system." (p. 317.)

Chapter 3

1. Satir (1971) discusses the double bind. The conditions are: the person being "bound" receives strong conflicting messages from a survival figure (someone on whom he/she is physically or emotionally dependent). That is, one message is received at one level of communication, and a simultaneous message is contradictory at another level. Other observations made in families with schizophrenic members are things like:

[1] Little use of personal pronouns or first names.
[2] They rarely look directly at one another while speaking.
[3] They often sound or look incongruent with what they say.

A fundamental clinical observation in diagnosing families who present symptomatic children is that the symptom is a sign that this family's rules conflict with the requirements of human life. (pp. 663-670.)

2. Haley (1963) defines psychopathology in an individual as a product of the way he deals with intimate relations; the way they deal with him, and the ways other family members involve him in their relationships with one another. Symptomatic behavior, from this standpoint, perpetuates a family system. Contrasting this with traditional approaches rooted in psychoanalysis, Haley cites that the function of symptoms in this case was to maintain an intrapsychic

balance. Family relations were considered secondary to the problems confronting the analyst. Conflict in an individual was understood to be conflict between intrapsychic impulses and drives that are repressed by societal forces. A power struggle within the individual was the formal theme of treatment. For Haley, conflict is envisioned as occurring outside the person and in the context of his actual relationships. "Psychopathology is a product of a power struggle between persons rather than between internal forces." The major shift in psychiatric theory is explained as follows: "external conflicts induce inner ones which reflect them." (p. 156.) A cybernetic theoretical concept is proposed as a model through which treatment strategies can develop. The fundamental issue, defined as a struggle for power, is then posed as a therapeutic question—how might the therapist devise therapeutic tactics for resolving power struggles?

Haley analyzes communication in order to interpret rigid dysfunctional patterns. Identifying the dysfunctional coalitions in the family system, the therapist uses himself as a mediator and agent of change to disrupt these coalitions. For example, Haley (1963) writes, "By not responding on the patient's terms when the patient is exhibiting symptomatic or distressful behavior, the therapist requires the patient to deal with him in other ways, in both individual and family therapy." (p. 171.)

Minuchin's (1974) work is similar. Unlike individual psychodynamically oriented therapy, he believes that the therapeutic use of the self is of utmost importance. "Change," according to Minuchin, "is seen as occurring through the process of the therapist's affiliation with the family and his restructuring of the family in a carefully planned way, so as to transform dysfunctional transactional patterns." (p. 91.) Watzlawick, Weakland, and Fisch (1974) similarly focus upon what is going on, carefully avoiding why questions. "These techniques deal with effects and not their presumed causes; the crucial question is what? and not why?" (p. 83.) An exaggerated view of family systems theory is cited by Ferber and Ronz (1972) where they write, "a behavioral system is composed of behaviors, not persons. . . . To describe this system, we focus on behaviors, their patterns of occurrences and integrative relationships." (p. 357.) Again, the method is to take sides in order to disrupt pathogenic relationships. Little attempt is made toward clarifying the socio-political source of the conflict itself. In each case, the therapeutic goal is to restructure the family so that they can live more harmoniously and responsively to the various changes and challenges that they must face as a unit in the social order.

3. Minuchin (1974), active in treating psychosomatic disorders, presents a case of a 12-year old girl with asthma which was psychosomatically triggered. Changing the structure of the family patterns by moving two overprotective parents to care, not only for the asthmatic child, but also for their other daughter who was obese, interrupted the asthmatic sysmptoms of the 12-year-old. (p. 13.)

From a socio-political perspective, one can understand that the overprotectiveness of both parents to one child may have been influenced by a myriad of social myths and pressures. Poor attendance in school often is reinterpreted by parents as a failing on their part and in response, believing that school is of utmost importance, pressure upon the child to attend regularly exacerbates her condition. There are numerous other ways one can explain the social effects impinging upon the family. Yet, there is a serious psychosomatic problem which requires immediate attention concerning the infrastructure of family patterns and the effect of these patterns upon symptom production.

REFERENCES

Ackerman, N. W. *The Psychodynamics of Everyday Life.* New York: Basic Books, 1958.

Ackerman, N. W. Family therapy. In S. Arieti (Ed.), *American Handbook of Psychiatry,* vol. III. New York/London: Basic Books, 1966, p. 209.

Altbach, E.H. *Women in America.* Mass.: D. C. Heath & Co., 1974.

Aldous, J. Occupational characteristics and male's role performance in the family. *Journal of Marriage and Family,* 1969, *31,* 707-713.

Aries, P. The family; Prison of love. *Psychology Today,* Aug. 1975, pp. 53-58.

Auerswald, H. Interdisciplinary versus ecological approach. *Family Process,* 1968, *7*(2), 202-215.

Axelson, L. Marital adjustment and marital role definitions of working and non-working wives. *Marriage and Family Living,* 1963, *25,* 189-195.

Bales, R. Glencoe, Ill.: The Free Press, 1955.

Barber, B. R. *Liberating Feminism.* New York: The Seabury Press, 1975.

Bauman, K. E. Relationship between age at first marriage, school dropout, and marital instability: An analysis of the Glick Effect. *Journal of Marriage and the Family,* Nov. 1967, pp. 672-680.

Bell, J. E. Recent advances in family group therapy. *Journal of Child Psychology and Psychiatry,* 1962, pp. 1-15.

Bell, W., & Vogel, E. Toward a framework for functional analysis of family behavior. *A Modern Introduction to the Family.* Illinois: The Free Press of Glencoe, 1960, pp. 1-36.

Bernard, J. The paradox of the happy marriage. In V. Gornick & B. K. Moran (Eds.), *Women in a Sexist Society: Studies in power and powerlessness.* New York: Basic Books, 1971.

Blood, R., & D. M. Wolfe. *Husbands and Wives: The Dynamics of Married Life.* Illinois: Glencoe Free Press, 1960.

Boszormenyi-Nagy, I., & J. L. Framo. (Eds.). *Intensive Family Therapy,* New York: Harper & Row, 1965.

Bowen, M. Family psychotherapy. *American Journal of Orthopsychiatry,* 1961, *31*(1), 40-60.

Bratter, T. E. Wealthy families and their drug abusing adolescents. *Journal of Family Counseling,* Spring, 1975, *3*(1), 62-76.

Bronfenbrenner, V. *American Families: Trends and Pressures. Hear-*

ings Before the Senate Subcommittee on Children and Youth of the Committee on Labor and Public Welfare. United States Senate, 43rd Congress, 1st Session. Sept. 24, 25, 26, 1973. Washington, D.C.: Government Printing Office, 1973.

Broverman, I. K., Broverman, D. M., Clarkson, F. E., Rosenkrantz, P. S., & Vogel, S. R. Sex-role stereotypes and clinical judgments of mental health. *Journal of Consulting and Clinical Psychology,* 1970, 34, 1-7.

Burgess, E. W. From Colonial family to the family of the future. In Ruth Cavan (Ed.), *Marriage and Family in the Modern World.* New York: Thomas Y. Cromwell, Co., 1960, pp. 58-63.

Chesler, P. Marriage and psychotherapy. *The Radical Therapist.* New York: Ballentine Books, 1971, pp. 175-180.

Chesler, P. *Women and Madness.* Garden City, New York: Doubleday, 1972.

Clements, W. H. Marital intervention and marital stability: A point of view and a descriptive comparison of stable and unstable marriages. *Journal of Marriage and the Family,* November 1967, pp. 770-772.

Cowhig, J. D. Marital instability among women in the United States. *Welfare in Review,* July 1965, pp. 12-14.

Cutler, B. R., & Dyer, W. G. Initial adjustment processes in young married couples. *Social Forces,* December 1965, pp. 195-201.

Deckard, B. *The Women's Movement: Political, Socioeconomic and Psychological Issues.* New York: Harper & Row, 1975.

Eisenstein, V. W. *Neurotic Intervention in Marriage.* New York: Basic Books, 1956.

Farrell, W. *The Liberated Man.* New York: Random House, 1974.

Farson, R. *Birth Rights.* New York: Macmillan, 1974.

Fischer, J. The Mental Research Institute on Family Therapy. *Family Therapy,* 1974, *1*(2), 105-140.

Firestone, S. *The Dialectic of Sex: The Case for Feminist Revolution.* New York: Bantom Books, 1970.

Ferber, A., & J. Ranz. How to succeed in family therapy: Set reachable goals—Give workable tasks. In C. J. Sager & H. S. Kaplan (Eds), *Progress in Group and Family Therapy.* New York: Brunner Mazel, 1972, pp. 346-384.

Ferree, M. M. The confused American housewife. *Psychology Today,* Sept. 1976, *10*(4), 76-78.

Fleck, S. Family dynamics and origin of schizophrenia. *Psychosomatic Medicine,* 1960, *22*, 333.

Framo, L. The theory of the technique of family treatment of schizophrenia. *Family Process,* 1962, *1*, 119-131.

Friedman, P. H. Outline (alphabet) of 26 techniques of family and marital therapy: A through Z. *Psychotherapy: Theory, Research & Practice,* 1974, *11,* 3.

Gager, N. (Ed.). *Womens Rights Almanac.* Bethesda: Elizabeth Cady Stanton Publ.Co., 1974.

Gibson, G. Kin family networks: Overheralded structure in past conceptualizations of family functioning. *Journal of Marriage and the Family,* 1972, *34*(1), 13-23.

Goodman, D. The whole and wholesome family: Your hope and the hope of America. In H. L. Silverman (Ed.), *Mental Therapy: Psychological, Sociological and Moral Factors.* Chicago: Charles C. Thomas Publisher, 1972, pp. 318-331.

Goodsell, W. *A History of the Family as a Social and Educational Institution.* New York: MacMillan Co., 1926.

Gornick, V. Consciousness. *The New York Times Magazine,* January, 1971, p. 10.

Gough, K. Is the family universal—the Nayar case. *Journal of the Royal Anthropological Institute,* 1959, *39,* part 1.

Greer, G. *The Female Eunuch.* New York: McGraw Hill, 1970.

Group for the Advancement of Psychiatry, Committee on the Family. Intergrations and mal-integrations in American middle class family patterns. 1968, *6*(27A), 697-979.

Haley, J. *Strategies of Psychotherapy.* New York: Grune & Stratton, 1963.

Haley, J. *Problem Solving Therapy.* San Francisco: Jossey Bass, 1976.

Hanisch, C. The personal is political. *The Radical Therapist.* New York: Ballantine Books, 1971, pp. 152-157.

Harland, M. *Making Home Life Attractive.* New York: The University Society, 1902.

Henry, J. *Culture Against Man.* New York: Vintage Books, 1965.

Hess, R. D., & J. V. Torney. *The Development of Political Attitudes in Children.* New York: Anchor Books, Doubleday & Company, 1968.

Howells, J. G. The nuclear family as the functional unit in psychiatry. *Child Psychiatry Quarterly,* 1971, *4,* 3-4, 7-18.

Howells, J. G. *Theory and Practice of Family Psychiatry.* New York: Brunner Mazel, 1971.

Isbister, C. The Family, past present and future. *Medical Journal of Australia* (Sidney), 1973, *1*(15), 762-764.

Jackson, D. D. "The question of family homeostasis. *Psychiatric Quarterly Supplement,* 1957, *31,* 79-90.

Jackson, D. D. "The study of the family. *Family Process,* 1965, *4,* 1-20.

Jaffe, D. T. Therapy Types: Bureaucrats, Healers, and Communities.

In *Journal of Humanistic Psychology,* Spring 1976, *16,* 3, 15-28.

Janeway, E. *Between Myth and Morning: Women Awakening.* New York: William Morrow, 1974.

Koch, J., & L. Koch. The urgent drive to make good marriages better. *Psychology Today,* Sept. 1976, *10*(4), 33-35.

Koprowski, R. J. Business technology and the American family: An impressionistic analysis. *Family Coordinator,* 1973, *22*(2), 229-234.

Kluckhohn, C. "Variations in the human family. *The Family in a Democratic Society.* New York: Columbia Press, 1949, pp. 3-11.

Kunnes, R. How to be a radical therapist. In *The Radical Therapist.* New York: Ballantine Books, 1971, pp. 27-34.

LaBarre, W. Appraising today's pressures on family living. *Social Casework,* 1951, *32,* 54-58.

L'Abate, L. Pathogenic role rigidity in fathers: Some observations. *Journal of Marriage and Family Counseling,* 1975, *1,* 1.

Laing, R. D. *The Politics of the Family and Other Essays.* New York: Pantheon Books, 1969, 1971.

Landrud, J. Moral values in the family. In H. L. Silverman (Ed.), *Marital Therapy.* Charles C. Thomas, 1972, pp. 362-371.

Lash, T. W., & H. Sigal. *State of the Child: New York City.* New York City: Foundation for Child Development, April 1976.

Laws, J. L. A feminist review of the marital adjustment literature: The rape of the Locke. *Journal of Marriage and the Family,* 1971, *33,* 483-516.

Lidy, T. Schizophrenia and the family. *Psychiatry,* 1958, *21,* 21.

Litwak, E. Three ways in which law acts as a means of social control. *Social Forces,* March 1956, *24,* 217-223.

Lowie, R. H. *Primitive Society.* New York, 1920, 66-67.

Mace, D. R. What I have learned about family life. *Family Coordinator,* 1974, *23*(2), 189-195.

Mander, A. V., & K. R. Rush. *Feminism as Therapy.* New York: Random House, 1974.

Marcuse, H. *One-Dimensional Man.* Boston: Beacon Press, 1964.

Mead, M. *Sex and Temperament in Three Primitive Societies.* New York, 1935.

Mercer, C. V. Interrelations among family stability, family composition, residence, and race. *Journal of Marriage and the Family,* August 1967, pp. 465-460.

Meyerowitz, J. H. Satisfaction during pregnancy. *Journal of Marriage and the Family,* Jan. 1970, *32,* 38-42.

Millet, K. *Sexual Politics.* New York: Doubleday and Co., Inc., 1970.

Mills, C. W. *The Power Elite*. New York: Oxford University Press, 1956.

Minuchin, S. *Families and Family Therapy*. Cambridge, Mass.: Harvard University Press, 1974.

Minuchin, S., Rosman, B. L., & Baker. L. *Psychosomatic Families: Anorexia nervosa in context*. Harvard University Press, 1978.

Nichols, J. *Men's Liberation: A New Definition of Masculinity*. New York: Penguin Books, 1975.

Olson, D. H. Marital and family therapy: Integrative review and critique. In C. B. Broderick (Ed.), *A Decade of Family Research and Action*. Minneapolis: National Council on Family Relations, 1970.

Orden, S. R., & N. M. Bradburn. Working wives and marriage happiness. *American Journal of Sociology*, Jan. 1969, pp. 392-407.

Parson, T. The stability of the American family system. In T. Parsons & F. Bales (Eds.), *Family, Socialization and Interaction Process*. Ill.: Glencoe Free Press, 1955, pp. 3-9.

Peitrofesa, J. J., & N. K. Schlossberg. *Counselor Bias and the Female Occupational Role*. Detroit: Wayne State University, 1970. (ERIC Document Reproduction Service No. CG 006 056)

Pinard, M. Marriage and divorce decisions and the larger social system: A case study in social change. *Social Forces*, March 1966, pp. 341-355.

Raush, L., Barry, A., Hertel, K., & M. Swain. *Communication Conflict and Marriage*. San Francisco: Jossey Bass, 1974.

Reich, W. *The Sexual Revolution*. New York, Farrar, Straus & Giroux, 1945.

Reich, W. *Character Analysis*. New York: Orgone Institute Press, 1949.

Renée, K. S. Correlates of dissatisfaction in marriage. *Journal of Marriage and the Family*, January 1970, pp. 54-66.

Rice, D., & J. K. Rice. Non-sexist marital therapy. *Journal of Marriage and Family Counseling*, Jan. 1977, *3*(1), 3-10.

Rogelio, D.-G. Neurosis and the Mexican family structure. *American Journal of Psychiatry*, 1955, *112*, 411-417.

Roszak, T. *The Making of a Counter Culture*. New York: Doubleday and Co., 1968.

Rowbotham, S. *Woman's Consciousness, Man's World*. England: Penguin Books, 1973.

Rubenstein, B. O., & Levitt, M. Some observations regarding the role of fathers in child psychotherapy. *Bulletin of the Menninger Clinic*, 1957, *21*, 16-27.

Rudikoff, S. Psychoanalysis and feminism. *Hudson Review,* Autumn 1975, *28*(3), 433-440.

Ruesch, J. Individual social techniques. *Journal of Social Psychology,* 1949, *29,* 3-28.

Ruesch, J., & G. Bateson. *Communication: The Social Matrix of Psychiatry.* New York: W. W. Norton Co., Inc., 1951, 1st ed.

Russell, B. *Marriage and morals.* New York: Horace Liveright, 1929.

Sarachild, K. Consciousness-raising and intuition. *The Radical Therapist.* New York: Ballantine Books, 1971, pp. 158-159.

Satir, V. *Conjoint Family Therapy.* New York: Science and Behavior Books, Inc., 1964.

Satir, V. Symptomatology: A family production in 1967. In J. G. Howells (Ed.), *Theory and Practice of Family Psychiatry.* New York: Burnner Mazel, 1971.

Scanzoni, J. A social system analysis of dissolved and existing marriages. *Journal of Marriage and the Family,* August 1968, *30,* 412-461.

Scott, R. D. Cultural frontiers in the mental health service. *Schizophrenia Bulletin,* Washington, D.C.: National Institute of Mental Health, 1974, *10,* 58-73.

Spiegel, J. The interplay between individual family and society. In J. J. Papa (Ed.), *Transactions.* New York: Science House, 1971.

Spiro, M. E. Is the family universal—The Israeli case. In N. Bell & E. Vogel (Eds.), *Modern Introduction to the Family.* Illinois: Free Press of Glencoe, 1960, pp. 54-75.

Steiner, C. Radical Psychiatry Principles. *The Radical Therapist.* New York: Ballantine Books, 1971. pp. 3-7.

Summer, W. G., & A. G. Keller. *The Science of Society.* New Haven: 1927, III, 1495-1498.

Szasz, T. S. The myth of mental illness. *The American Psychologist,* February 1960, *15,* 113-118.

Szasz, T. S. *Ideology and Insanity.* New York: Anchor Books, 1970.

Tec, N. Family and parenthood in contemporary American society. *Family Therapy,* 1975, *2*(3), 227-235.

The Radical Therapist. Produced by J. Agel. New York: Ballantine Books, 1971.

Thomas, A. H., & Stewart, N. R. Counselor response to females with deviate and conforming career goals. *Journal of Counseling Psychology,* 1971, *18*(4), 352-357.

Travis, C. Women: Work isn't always the answer. *Psychology Today,* Sept. 1976, *10*(4), 78.

Udky, R. J. Marital instability by race and income based upon 1960 Census data. *American Journal of Sociology,* May 1967, pp. 673-674.

Watzlawick, P., Weakland, J., & R. Fisch. Change principles *of Problem Formation and Problem Resolution.* New York: W. W. Norton and Co., Inc., 1974.

Weisstein, N. Psychology constructs the female. In V. Gornick & B. K. Maran (Eds.), *Women in a Sexist Society: Studies in Power and Powerlessness.* New York: Basic Books, 1971.

Wesley, C. The women's movement and psychotherapy. *Social Work,* March 1975, *20*(2), 120-125.

Whittaker, C. A. Psychotherapy with couples. *American Journal of Psychotherapy,* 1958, *12,* 18-23.

Whitehurst, R. N. Remarital reference—Group orientations and marriage adjustment. *Journal of Marriage and the Family,* August 1968, pp. 387-401.

Wilner, D., Walkey, R. P., Schram, J. M., Pinkerton, T. C., & M. Tayback. Housing as an environmental factor in mental health: The Johns Hopkins Longitudinal Study. *American Journal of Public Health,* 1960, *50*(1), 55-63.

Women's Rights Almanac. N. Gager. (Ed.). Bethesda, Maryland: Elizabeth Cady Station, 1974.

Weiner, N. *Cybernetics.* New York: Wiley, 1948.

Weiner, N. *The Human Use of Human Beings.*

Wynne, L. C. Pseudomutuality in the family relations of schizophrenia. *Psychiatry,* 1958, *21,* 205-220.

Young, K. What strong family life means to our society. *Social Casework, 1953, 34,* 323-329.

Zietz, D., & Erlich, J. L. Sexism in social agencies: Practitioners' perspectives. *Social Work,* November 1976, *21*(6), 434-439.

INDEX